Identity Theft

The False Inheritance
Exposing the Counterfeit God

CHERYL WESTON

Printed in the United States of America

Book Cover Design by Thomas Gonzalez, II
(Website: http://gonzalesdesign.com/)

Book Editor by Var Kelly of Var Ministries
(Email: VarMinistries@gmail.com)

DEDICATION

Although she has gone on to be with the Lord, the memories of seeing my grandma at the side of her bed praying night and day will remain in my faith files for the rest of my life. Therefore, I dedicate this book to one of Heaven's angels, Mrs. Olivia "Lilly" Gomes; to me you were the example of the Proverbs 31 Woman.

Grandma, thank you for introducing me to a man named Jesus.

TABLE OF CONTENTS

Dedication
Acknowledgments
Foreword
Preface

Introduction

ACKNOWLEDGEMENTS

To the One True and Living God, Yahweh. "Many there be which say of my soul, There is no help for him in God. Selah. But thou, O Lord, art a shield for me; my glory, and the lifter up of mine head." Psalms 3:2-3 (KJV)

Thank you, Father God, for hiding me in the cleft of the rock and for concealing me for such a time as this.

To Pastor Virgil and Prophetess Jean Johnson, I embrace you in The Spirit of Love. You celebrated with me when it was not your birthday.

To my family, thank you for loving Sam and Mary's only baby unconditionally.

To my clients at Fadez on 20th barbershop, Thank You for hanging in there with a Sista through MENOPAUSE! OMG!!! It is always my pleasure to groom you and redefine your image one cut at a time.

To my sister, Gerriettia Warr, you are the smile of heaven that lights up the darkest room. Don't lose this book!

To Prophetess Rhonda Corey-Davis, all I can say is COUSIN! You and Bishop Davis will never get rid of me.

To Bishop Kenneth L. Davis, aka pop, I submit! LOL!

To Minister Tauheedah Gomes, my favorite cousin; All I can say is… Loyalty. Loyalty. Loyalty.

To Margo Riggs, besides The Lord, I have never met a kinder person. I see you slaying 'em in the courtroom counselor!

To my BFF, Grace Lindsey. Every time I needed you, you were there and I love you deeply sis.

To my sis, Pastor Tanya Watts, God showed us everything we never want to become in ministry.

To Allison Williams - Who would have thought that a pair of Timberland boots would forged such a mighty prayer partnership? To God be The Glory.

To the late Bishop Sherwood Carthen, Thank you for daring to step out of religion and lay the foundation of what heaven's church should look like.

To Apostle Mary Lee Parker, your little mustard seed Word saved my life!

To Quinton Kelly, my brother the psalmist, your obedience to The TRUTH broke the chains. No and still NOOOOO! LOL!

To Dr. Andre Simms, my Washington pastor, you sir, are "The Bible Guy" for real. Your passion to preach the unadulterated TRUTH is un-comparable. Hope you're still enjoying the bow ties!

Thank you to everyone else; to all that prayed, called, texted, or stopped by the barbershop to bring an encouraging word, I love y'all.

FOREWORD

I met Cheryl in 2014 when she came to visit our church, Christ The King Bible Fellowship, in Federal Way, Washington. She was an inquisitive disciple who thoroughly knew The Bible. Chiefly, through her own brokenness and her desire to reach those within the church affiliated with the LGBTQ community, Cheryl displayed a great deal of passion, boldness, and fervency for The Lord.

Since I have known her, she has displayed a zeal for The Lord, biblical truth and discipline with love, truth and transparency.

If you are struggling with homosexuality, or know someone that can identify with the feeling of being stuck between biblical truth and societal norms that do not line up, or go against the truth, this book is for you.

As always, she delivers in her ability to keep it real, share the truth and extend an olive branch to those connected or disconnected from the body of Christ.

As a faithful and diligent student of The Scriptures, Cheryl has been blessed to be gifted with the ability to teach in a very black and white manner. She has the unique ability to reach the LBGTQ community with truth, without compromising, ostracizing, or alienating those she's trying to reach.

Cheryl's book is a remarkable testimony and one of many proven accounts that speak to God's ability to completely and totally deliver, transform, and set free!

This testimony proves that God is a healer to the wounded, comforter to the weeping, rest for the weary, guide for the lost, and restorer for the broken.

As you read this documented testimony, I would encourage you to leave enough room in your heart for God to show up and be God in your life!

Cheryl is a living witness that without God, nothing is possible, but with Him, nothing is impossible!

Heaven's Blessings,
Dr. Andre Sims,
Pastor & Founder of Christ The King Bible Fellowship (CKBF)
Federal Way, Washington

PREFACE

Greetings in the precious, loving and amazing name of The Lord Jesus Christ! All glory, honor, and praise to YAWEH, the one true God. My Papa. Redeemer. Healer. Deliver. Protector. Provider. Finder of the lost. Advocate for justice. Grace for the undeserving. Mighty conqueror. Comforter. The endless living water for the thirsty and the sustaining bread of life to all that are hungry. With all that is within my soul, I want to say thank you. Truly, you are The Lord of compassion and forgiveness, and The Shepherd of my soul. Your mercies are matchless and for this, I give you praise.

INTRODUCTION

Readers let me first begin by saying, Jesus got jokes and He has a sense of humor!

It's 3:00 pm on Sunday, February 4, 2018. The weather is so beautiful today. The temp is about seventy degrees with a small fall breeze that purposely slides in from the Bay Area, and cascades down the mountains to park itself in my hometown: Sacramento, California.

It's also Super Bowl Sunday, and instead of attending the hottest Super Bowl party with my BFF's Grace and Margo, where I can talk trash about my Aunty Kathy's Patriots, I'm in a hotel room adding the grammatical corrections to this testimony.

What is so hilarious is that I clearly remember telling God - after a failed investment of $3,500 dollars that I used to host an Identity Theft Conference that maybe 15 people showed up to - declaring to Him, "Check this out homie, nobody wants to hear this message. These are your sheep and if you want 'em saved, you God, SAVE THEM YOURSELF."

I can only imagine Jesus, compassionately laughing at my proclamation. I can see Him now, eating some hot buttered Holy Ghost Popcorn rocking back and forth in His majestic rocking chair saying, "Really Cheryl? Ewwww. I ain't scared of you!"

If you were to ask me if I believed that God would twelve years later fulfill His promise, honestly, I would have had to say no. I say that not because He's not a man of His word. The Word of God says, "So shall My Word be that goeth forth out of my mouth: it shall not return unto Me void, but it shall accomplish that which I please, and it shall prosper in the thing whereto I sent it" (Isaiah 55:11, KJV). I say no because I felt as if I failed God and my assignment.

Allow me to break it down to you and provide a little metaphor that is easy to conceptualize. Imagine you get a call from the President of the United States stating he wants to see you to discuss a Special Ops project that he wants you to oversee. Overjoyed with excitement, you rush to get all your clearances, hop on a flight to D.C. and within days you are seated and waiting in the Oval Office for the president to speak to you. Glancing around the room, your eyes catch hold of his many awards and honorary accomplishments which brings comfort, validation, and authenticity to his integrity and ability to lead the country as its commander-in-chief. Suddenly, he walks in and your heart is beating against your chest with excitement as he hands you the sealed white and gold confidential folder with the presidential seal. Inside it contains the outline of your assignment and he says, "I'm so glad you were able to agree to this assignment. Rest assured that with your specific skill set, you shall not fail."

Within seconds, and before you can ask any questions, the commander-in-chief shakes your hand and says, "I'm due in another meeting. I'll be in touch."

So, you're like, "Ok. Cool Mr. President thank you for the opportunity. I won't let you down, sir."

On the flight home, you begin reading over the outline. You are so juiced that the commander-in-chief called you and not only did he call you, he qualified you.

Everyone you share this experience with is ecstatic including yourself. You are so amped up that now you start feeling like a super hero and in your head, you start jamming to your own super hero theme song.

Days, weeks, and now months have passed and no word from Mr. Prez. By now, you have developed a slight attitude from waiting. Finally, you get the courage and call him on his main line. Unfortunately, he doesn't pick up. You leave a message and say, "I know your very busy running the country sir, however, I read over the outline several times and decided that I'll just move forward and save you the time of going over the small details. I got this, and I'll just take over from here. Holla back!" (Urban cultural phrase meaning call me back).

What you did not realize, had you patiently waited for him to return, was there were other strategic and vital components necessary to successfully complete your mission, and without the appropriate training that's needed for the assignment, you found yourself defeated, captured, and a prisoner of war.

Without going into the extended details of the 12 years since the publishing of this book - that's for another book - what echoes in the chambers of my soul are the words from the prophet Habakkuk that read, "For the vision is yet for an appointed time, but at the end it shall speak, and not lie: though it tarry, wait for it; because it will surely come, it will not tarry." (Habakkuk 2:3).

In my case, and regarding the complex and sensitive matter of faith and sexuality as it relates to SSA (same sex attraction), I left out the integral factor that pulls this testimony together - which the power of God will direct each reader to – is the unconditional love of Jesus, and His GRACE.

Whoever you are, whatever you have done, no matter how foul, how grimy, how low in the gutter, or what despicable strategies you constructed to climb the success ladder at the expense of another human being, I promise you, you are never beyond God's grace to save.

Along with grace, I have learned and come to understand the meaning of "appointed times and seasons." In speaking with my sister, Pastor Tamara Johnson, who tossed me a knowledge nugget she said, "Sis, you can be in a 'season' but it doesn't mean it's the 'appointed time'".

Earlier this year, I was grooming a client at Fadez on 20th barbershop and my co-worker and brother from another mother, Jalil, also dropped a nugget and said, "Sis, the sun shines on everything, but everything doesn't grow at the same time".

Talk about waiting on God's appointed time!

Let's look at a few biblical characters where it seemed like God took His time to fulfill His word:

- Poor old Noah and his family building an ark for 120 years in 90-degree weather while every other campsite is eating BBQ, sippin' on cold Heinekens and turning up to Drake. Everyone mocked and laughed at him, until it began to rain. (Genesis 6:13-22)
- Seven years after Samuel anointed David, David sat on the throne as the king of Israel. (1Samuel 16:1-13)
- Abraham's wife Sarah, barren, and well past the years of being able to have kids, at the age of 90, gives birth, and delivers Isaac. (Genesis 21:1-3.)
- In addition, Ecclesiastes 3:1 says, "To everything there is a season, a time for every purpose under heaven"

I am confident in knowing that for every failed lesson, every difficult trial, every slammed door, and every jagged knife that penetrated deep into my soul, and every tear I cried from betrayal, was all God's divine setup for His will and appointed time and is now working for my good and His glory (Romans 8:28). In fact, God used this platform as a type of metrics to polish and refine my skills for this assignment.

The Lord used the gentleness of His Holy Spirit and long-suffering, (2 Peter 2:8), which left his indelible imprint upon my heart, that testifies to the depths of just how far Jesus will go, to save, reconcile and restore a sinner. Amen.

CHAPTER 1: MY GENDER IDENTITY

From the floor up, my identity and swagger were defined by what I wore and how I rocked it. From a casual perspective, I had to slide into a fresh pair of cocaine-white Nike Air Force Ones, a Macy's Alfani t-shirt, and a little sag from my Balenciaga designer jeans so women could get a glance at the matching Alfani boxers. On my wrist, I sported a platinum Invicta watch with the matching necklace and bracelet. I wore my red and white New York Yankees lid (baseball hat) slightly low on my forehead and a blunt behind my diamond-studded ear.

On the flip side, when I was ready for the takedown, my evening attire consisted of a tailored-to-fit Kenneth Cole suit, Kenneth Cole dress shirt, Jacquard silk bow tie, Paul Smith designer socks, Jimmy Choo boots, and a splash of Paco Rabanne.

To secure the takedown (sex) I listened intensively to her subtle pleasures and strategically laid my traps. Always, my main objective on any date was to create the atmosphere that left no room for escape.

I was a Boss, player, hustler, charismatic Don extraordinaire who could manipulate the wedding ring off a woman's finger before she took her last bite of filet Mignon. I was the never-on-the-bottom, thug-passion-lover, stud–for-real, and they called me "Big Nasty."

I took pride in "turning out" heterosexual women, especially the ones who proclaimed, "I'm strictly into men, but honey if I wasn't, you would be the one." I cannot count the times I had to ask those type of women the question, "…and how do you like your eggs in the morning?"

I smoked weed, snorted coke, drank tequila, and manipulated The Word of God. Hear me reader, for over thirty years I was solid in the game; I walked the walk and talked the talk.

I started sneaking into gay bars, using false I.D. at age eighteen.

My identity, already established, allowed the femes (feminine lesbians) to know I was Daddy. In my younger days, all the studs (masculine women) would hang out downtown at the gay bar getting crump (amped up) because Wednesday night was Ladies Night, and Sistas were choosing. Sunday afternoons was the Tea Dance, and I cannot recall ever leaving the club without a pocket full of numbers I never called. My rule was they had to call me Daddy. Sacramento's lesbian scene was the beginning platform for me to sharpen my game.

As my swag developed, I knew that beyond Sacramento's borders, were a cornucopia of beautiful women, and I was on a mission to "go fishing."

In the late 90's, my stud partners and I drove to the Bay Area to party with thousands of other lesbians at San Francisco's Gay Pride Weekend. I remember standing on the hill and looking down into the jovial streets of San Francisco's Castro District; I'll never forget what I saw. There were families, toddlers and adolescent kids of gay and lesbian partners dancing and rejoicing. Thousands upon thousands waving gay pride flags. I witnessed people of every race, creed and color of humanity full of jubilee at their sexual liberation.

As I continued to walk the parade route, loud techno music resounded from the open doors of overcrowded gay bars. Men, women, Transvestites, Drag Queens; I mean all types of people were dancing in the streets and on top of cars. Lovers in corner cafes, decorative tables with pamphlets from organizations who were there to support every crisis the homosexual could encounter. While vendors sold gay pride bracelets, shirts, shoes, maps, stickers, etc., the chapters for AIDS Awareness Organizations gave out free pamphlets and free testing. I was in awe and overwhelmed by the experience.

In hindsight, the best way to describe it would be a passage from the book of Revelations that states, "I saw a number that no man could number." (Revelations 7:9).

I met lawyers, doctors, politicians, entrepreneurs, and teachers. I thought, "We are everywhere; we are a nation."

Hello reader, my name is Cheryl Weston. I'm an only child born in Sacramento, California to Samuel and Mary Weston, and I've had a successful career as a master barber. The following is a factual account and testimony of my lifestyle as a lesbian and my deliverance through the love of God.

In my mind, the only biblical ties that could allegorically suggest the miracle of this deliverance was my father's name was Samuel and my mother's name was Mary. To my knowledge, there are no Preachers, Prophets, Pastors, Bishops, Apostles, Evangelists, Theologians, or Scholars in my family. As a child, I have no recollection of being raped by a man or woman. My father never physically or emotionally hit or abused my mother. I have never had an intimate sexual relationship with a man. I am a virgin with my hymen intact and currently practicing celibacy, by choice. In fact, my current occupation is a master barber and I pride myself on my career and the amazing, wonderful, healthy relationships I have with men from all backgrounds. I have no history of molestation. Love and respect were high moral values in my home and I lacked neither. Despite what society has constructed as "normal" I lived an amazing life full of love and rich in culture.

However, I identified myself as lesbian.

CHAPTER 2: MY MOTHER'S SON

My dad was from New Orleans. A tall, handsome man mixed with French and Creole. His debonair, suave, and gift of gab is what hooked my mom, line and sinker. I admired several things about my dad, like is work ethic, respect for his family, calm spirit, and chivalry. He served in the US Navy and while serving overseas, a tattoo artist tatted the Virgin Mary on his whole back. His artistic gift graced him to create amazing abstract art including paintings, sketches, and even woodcarvings. He could pick up a piece of wood laying on the side of the road and turn it into an amazing piece of art. I mean, the brotha had gifts! He dressed meticulously, smelled heavenly, and had the coldest walk this side of the Mississippi.

As a little girl, I would always watch him lay out his clothes and I am sure now, this is where I picked up my swag because he was a meticulous dresser.

I was in awe of my Dad. After my parents left to go and hang with their friends, I would sneak into their bathroom, grab his tooth brush pretending it was his razor. I would apply his shaving cream to my face, and imitate what I had seen him do by moving it over my cheeks, using similar motions. I even tried to imitate his look by applying his Murrays pomade to my hair and parting it on the side like his. I wanted to be like my dad so badly that I would practice standing up while I urinated. I remember catching it one morning from my mom. My dad sat on the couch without a shirt, so I thought it would be cool if I did the same. Of course, I got my tail whooped. That put a halt to the "no shirt" phase. I never saw myself as my mother's daughter. Rather, more like her son.

I loved everything about men. I loved their walk, their conversation, the sound of their voices; which I could imitate, especially early in the mornings. I especially loved the design of their bodies. I became a gym rat and worked out religiously just to create big arms, big shoulders and a big chest. When I could see the results and definition in my chest, I would call it my 'nest.' Although I have never been with a man sexually, I was mesmerized with their penis because of the power it possessed in controlling women's emotions.

I had plenty of male cousins and clients and unbeknownst to them, I studied them day and night. My career as a barber provided the platform to research men of all social and economic backgrounds. Some were athletes, pimps, players, gangsters, family men, businesspersons, and pastors. I acquainted myself with their mannerisms, studied their habits and characteristics until the outward manifestation was complete. I transformed my environment, mind, and my heart until it reflected what I had believed I was. My now androgynous appearance served well my new identity, and society no longer viewed me as a woman.

While my mother was beautiful, I had no desire to be like her. I wanted, however, to date women as beautiful as her. My mother, in the opinion of many, was the backbone of our family. She cooked, cleaned, held down two jobs, balanced the finances and made it work. Every chance she got, she made sure I was prepared and equipped to take on life's challenges.

Like I did with my dad, I would also watch my mother as she prepared for work. She dressed professionally, smelled heavenly, and her make-up was flawless. Frankly her only imperfection (and it was major to me) was her controlling attitude. My mother had to control everything in my life. She told me what to wear and how and when to wear it. She taught me how young women should walk, talk, and sit. She drilled me repeatedly on how to properly dine at the dinner table should a man one day come a-courting!

Once, for church, my mother dressed me in a beautiful yellow dress with a white petticoat, matching yellow ribbons in my hair, black patent leather shoes and a matching bag, honey. You could not tell me I wasn't the fairest of them all! Skipping down the street like Little Red Riding Hood, I go to show off my pretty little dress to my friends who were sitting in a tree chilling, and let me tell you, they laughed so hard and talked about my little yellow dress and sent me home crying like a baby. (Just so wrong!) When I got in the house, I yelled for my mother and I shouted at the top of my voice, "TAKE THIS UGLY DRESS OFF ME, NOW!"

Eighteen years later, I think I put on another dress. As I grew, my thoughts were centered on reaching that age of accountability— "being grown" —so that I could get out of my mother's house.

Life was tough being my parent's only child. My mom was controlling and a protective mama bear that will bite the head off anybody who tried to hurt her baby girl. However, I vowed when the opportunity came for me to get my own crib, I would never let another woman control my life. I would be the "HNIC." (Head Negro in Charge).

At night, while lying in bed, I would tell God that I think He made a mistake because surely, I should have been born a boy. As I began to drift asleep, I deeply gazed at the wedding picture of my parents and dreamt of my own wedding. There I stood flossin' in my tuxedo, thick Mack Daddy and fine as wine. Standing by my side was my beautiful wife and she was flawless from the crown of her head, all the way down to her stilettos. As I think back to those times, I believe it was then, that Satan began to plant the seed, whereas God has provided now the revelation, covertness.

CHAPTER 3: THE FIRST MIRACLE

My grandmother, as far as I can remember, never missed Sunday mass and baby let me tell you, if I was not able to pull it together or if I played hooky from church, trust and believe, there were no smiles, hugs, or snacks after dinner until she decided to forgive! Grandma would say, "There is absolutely no reason to miss church!" She also would say, "You mean to tell me you can't give The Lord forty-five minutes of your time?" I thank God that my grandmother introducing me to Jesus. This introduction led to my first encounter with The Lord.

One day the gate to my backyard was open and my dog, Peanuts, ran away. This was the first dog I ever owned and my soul companion. I was about nine years old, and I remember my grandmother, more than likely tired of hearing me cry say, "Cheryl, pray that Jesus brings him home." What else is there for a little girl to do but try everything she knew to find her best friend? I didn't even know my grandmother's God, nor had I talked to Him or knew if He would talk back. The only point of reference was the picture I had seen on statues and the one hanging in the hallway. As I laid on the coach with eyes full of tears, I remembered the big gold Catholic Bible under the coffee table. I placed my hands on it and prayed, "Jesus, please bring my dog back home." The next day, my cousin Mark called, saying, "I found your dog." This was the first of many prayers that The Lord would answer.

As my hunger grew to know my grandmother's Jesus, ironically, so did my male identity. Little by little, I was becoming comfortable with being gay. In fact, I can recall being at various markets or shopping centers, and when browsing through the stores, the salesperson would approach me and ask, "Can I help you, sir?" I would chuckle and think to myself, "I fooled you again."

CHAPTER 4: A SEARCH FOR MEANING

In my early teens, I began to question the validity of the Catholic religion. I wondered why the Father (Priest) would read from the whole Bible and we only got a pamphlet. I asked myself, "Why do I have to enter a wooden box to confess my sins?" I also wondered if the confessional box was confidential and private. When the priest slid the little door open to speak to me I wondered, "Can he see me?" If he could see me, God forbid, and recognized me, my confessions, which included my having done some terrible things, would probably not be confidential, and the exposure would result in a sore behind from my grandmother and maybe even rejection.

I asked Grandma many questions regarding Catholicism and her response was, "You should never question The Lord." I remember during the Season of Lent, in preparation for Easter, all of the television stations would air biblically based movies like The Ten Commandments, The Robe and The Story of Jesus of Nazareth. I loved watching the movies especially Jesus of Nazareth, I mean that guy was so dope. He healed the sick, gave sight to the blind, raised the dead, put ears back on - so who wouldn't want to be #TeamJesus right?

I would say to myself, "I love that man called Jesus." Time evolved and eventually I grew up and I wanted more information than what the Catholic religion could offer me about Jesus. Yet, at the same time, my love for women was growing as well.

CHAPTER 5: HEARING THE VOICE OF THE LORD

In 1984, my mother was diagnosed with Chronic Obstructive Pulmonary Disease (CPOD). My mother tried her best to continue to work and provide for her family, but eventually she had to retire from the State of California and her battle to survive began.

I had graduated high school and faded in and out of the church scene. My grandmother had moved to Boston to live the rest of her life with my aunt and her family. The absence of her presence and her leadership were now faded memories that were unable to arrest my rebellion. I was finding my way in the gay lifestyle and each female partner massaged my confidence. I was becoming a true player, and my swag was being stoked like a Christmas fire. I was becoming popular in the gay community. I stayed fly and had a standing Friday appointment with my barber to keep that taper fresh (type of hair cut).

Years had passed by now, and my mother's disease was growing progressively worse. My mother's dependence upon me grew as well. I have to admit, this had to be the very darkest time of my life. I was in my mid-twenties, and right before my eyes the woman who had been my rock was dying and deteriorating. My father picked up heroin use overseas and struggled with his addiction, unable to care for me. Eventually heroin's cycle had sunken its talons deep into my father's soul and he abandoned us.

As a debonair young stud in the prime of my life, relentlessly feeding my sexual appetite slowly became a faded dream, as the reality of my mother's condition and my father's abandonment left me to become my mother's sole caretaker. It was the height of the 90's and homosexuality became less of a societal weight. I landed an excellent job in healthcare, worked full-time and attended junior college part-time.

Sadly, my mother's disease progressed and on top of COPD, another fatal blow came with another diagnosis: emphysema and CHF (congestive heart failure). The doctor informed me that less than 20 percent of my mother's lungs were functioning. My mother regularly ingested at least thirteen pills a day, and these pills only added more problems for her. The side effects were hallucinations and mood swings. Watching my mother in this condition made me feel hopeless, powerless, and led to severe depression.

COPD is horrible. The disease restricted my mom's bronchial tubes. She was unable to get a full breath. The nights when I heard her struggling to breathe were complete torture. Unlike recovering from the pain from a surgery where you can take a pill and ease the discomfort, I could not give my mother breath. I cannot remember how many ER rides I went on and the emergency calls at work that left my PTO bank drained. On one occasion, it was so bad; her doctor admitted her into ICU.

I had to manage our home, but I had never seen nor paid a bill. These responsibilities were new to me. I could not locate the account number, let alone pay the bill.

I recall walking home from softball practice and finding my father and another man shooting up heroin at our kitchen table. Respect in the Cabo Verde culture was a mandate, however, that night I cussed him out so bad I am sure he wanted to crawl back into his mama's womb, never wanting to be born. Doing a little detective work, something led me to go into the spare bedroom and flip over the mattress and what I discovered were checks, cash, and needles. My father had wiped out our checking and savings accounts and for a while, he was MIA.

Still struggling from her ICU bed, my mother asked, "Where is your father?" Tears rolled down my eyes, and I did not have the heart to tell her what I had witnessed, and that he had disappeared.

God strengthened my mother and after a few weeks, her doctor moved her into a regular room. Intuitively, she knew I was alone and afraid. She understood the loyalty and love I felt for my dad, which compelled me to cover his betrayal. My mother's will to survive and protect her only child was the remedy that strengthened her so that she was finally able to leave the hospital. However, by now, our home was in foreclosure, our cars repossessed, and we were flat broke.

Driven by the little knowledge I had gained from my earlier readings of The Bible and my childhood experience, it felt as if an unseen force was whispering, "Don't throw in the towel." I prayed to my grandma's Jesus night and day, begging him to send someone to help us. I searched for a miracle, but none came, nor did it seem that God had heard my prayers. From what I heard some say in The Bible regarding God and gays, it led me to believe that because I was gay, I had become invisible to The Lord and damned to Hell. However, just as I was thinking the worst about God, my Aunty Barbra Corey showed up. She cooked, cleaned, did our shopping and shared The Gospel of Jesus Christ with us. And suddenly, as if God heard my cry, I got a telephone call. A lesbian friend had recently accepted Jesus Christ and invited me to church. Friends had previously invited me to visit some Baptist churches, but coming from Catholic solemnity to Baptist sensationalism, was quite a cultural shock. I loved the music but was petrified of their "whooping" preaching style.

It was New Year's Eve, 1985, and my friend brought me to her church. When the Pastor began to speak, it was as if God had heard my every prayer and seen each tear that had fallen from my eyes. I began to cry uncontrollably as He spoke. I felt a presence that seemed to engulf me. I knew that this minister had all the answers to every question I had asked my grandma about Jesus. Suddenly, he stopped his dissertation and said, "Every head bowed, every eye closed, and every saint of God praying." The still silence was as if God had demanded that Heaven and Earth freeze. I remember hearing the pastor say, "Jesus loves you and if today, you want to make Jesus Christ your personal savior, raise your hand." My hand flew up immediately. He went on to say, "For those of you who have your hand up, please bring your personal belongings with you, we have a staff person in the back that wants to pray with you."

Baby, I ran down that aisle and I know I looked like a sprinter in the 40-yard dash.

My mother noticed a dramatic change in my behavior almost instantly. I told her I had been saved and showed her my new Bible (I minister with that same Bible today). Under the leadership of this Pastor, I learned how to pray, worship and study The Bible. God began to restore our lives and restore to my mother the joyous life that her sickness tried to rob her of. As a benefit, a Cabo Verde fundraiser dance raised $1,000, which helped us get back on our feet. That financial seed enabled us to rent a two-bedroom apartment because our house and cars were no more. My uncle gave us a green 1972 Delta Oldsmobile.

I needed to call "X" from the show "trick my ride" to help a Sista out. No matter how many car fresheners I used, I could not get rid of the mildew smell.

The torn fabric lining in the ceiling dripped corrosive dust on my head and I always needed to cover it like a hijab. The driver's side door never did open, so I had to roll the window down to let myself out, but hey, it had an engine and I could get to work and church.

I remember my mom once saying, "When you're in your room praying, it sounds like you're fighting against the devil." By now, filled with The Holy Ghost and with the evidence of speaking in tongues, I was on fire for The Lord. I worshipped, prayed and rebuked the devil in the name of Jesus. I was turning into a little prayer warrior. As I grew in the knowledge of The Lord, I eventually served in the youth ministry as youth counselor. I had been attending church for about 18 months and every chance I got, I spoke about the wonderful things that God had done for my mother and me.

One Friday night after I stood before the church and gave my testimony, the church erupted with praise and The Holy Spirit moved so mightily that there was not a dry eye was in the house. Shortly after, I was approached by a strange woman who lightly touched my shoulder, just enough to get my attention. Pulling me to the side and away from the previous conversation I was having, she said, "Sister, you don't know who I am, but I was sent by The Lord to tell you that you are on your road to evangelism." I did not understand at that time just what evangelism was, so I said, "Give me a sec." I returned to my group. She spoke with such assurance and authority that I excused myself from the other conversation to ask her to clarify her statement. When I turned around, she was no longer there. No one else had seen this woman, and the ushers told me that no one had come in or out of the foyer for about twenty minutes. I ran out to the parking lot of the church to look around, but she was gone, and I never saw this woman again.

CHAPTER 6: FULL CIRCLE

For many nights, I could not get the word "evangelist" out of my head. While I slept, I would often dream of preaching. I even started to mimic my pastor by preaching to my imaginary congregation in my bedroom.

As a young believer, I thought that once saved, the devil was unable to entice me, nor did he have the power to lure me with what had enslaved me. I loved Jesus. Yet, I still struggled with my attraction to women.

During a Wednesday night Bible study, she was walking down the stairs as I was walking up. I never saw the enemy coming. When we passed each other, time stood still and in that very moment, I looked into that Sista's eyes and quietly affirmed to my flesh that she had to be the most beautiful woman I had ever seen.

Later, we would meet again on those same stairs on our way to Wednesday night Bible study. We shared casual conversations and passive eye contact and eventually, we exchanged phone numbers. Today, this woman walks in complete deliverance so to protect her identity, I will just call her Beautiful.

Beautiful owned a 1978 Burgundy Chevrolet that started when it wanted to. Beautiful hit me up one day and asked if I had AAA Insurance or if I could give her a jump. Without hesitation, I jumped in my ride and was on my way. I prepped myself all the way to her house saying, "You can do this Cheryl: Resist, Resist, Resist."

No need to call AAA, because that old school Chevy started right up with some jumper cables I had in the trunk. The Lord had just blessed me with a brand new, fresh-off-the-showroom-floor, white Hyundai, with blue interior with all the bells and whistles. Just when I thought that I had the victory, I shut the trunk and turned to get into my car when, "Woosh!" All the pep talk flew right out the door and with her sweet seductive voice she said, "Would you like to come in? I cooked." Man, my flesh spun me around so fast I was dizzy and tripped on the porch steps trying to get inside.

Our affair was brief, ending with my mother walking into my bedroom and catching us in a compromising position. My mom was so devastated and confused that she called our pastor. We were exposed and humiliated. Neither of us returned to that church for many years after that. The weight of the guilt of sin and our exposure was overwhelming and far too great for a new believer to bear.

I tried hard to conceal my feelings for women, but eventually they became feelings of resentment and bitterness for God and His church. I began to question God about my purpose and destiny.

Once I asked God a question. I said, "If man was given free will, what kind of choice is free when to choose one thing over the other causes damnation?" I thought, what's free about that? I became miserable and, in my misery, I started to research other religions and philosophies. Since I did not hear form God concerning my petition, impatience and idleness set in, and my mission and new purpose was to avenge my brokenness. I researched every book that would prove a false authenticity of the King James Bible. I dabbled in metaphysics, scientology, astrology, and joined the Pan African movement.

My research led to the historic continent of Egypt and I launched my studies in its rich history and culture. The information I discovered was priceless. I joined the local Pan African Church and indulged myself in their customs and rituals. However, because I knew The Holy Spirit a little bit, something was wrong, and my spirit could sense it. Although the culture and experience were rich, I knew my Heavenly Father's voice and the presence of His Holy Spirit was not in that place.

Pressing my way through the frustration and painful memories of being exposed, I relentlessly moved forward on my quest to find a religion that would accept my lifestyle.

Eventually I met a friend who introduced me to Buddhism. I found that the principles were like those of Christianity, so I found the transition to be an easy one. For example, instead of praying to one God for "blessings," you were a god and chanted for "benefits." However, I still felt a spiritual void, and faintly I would hear this still small voice inside calling to me. Many times, I would sit in front of my Gohonzon and just stare into it hoping it would talk back to me like Jesus did.

Nevertheless, I kept chanting until one night, I heard the spirit of The Lord Jesus say, "Why are you worshiping another god? Why have you bowed yourself before this graven image? If you deny Me before men, I will deny you before My Father in Heaven."

I stood straight up, and I was shaking in my skin. I looked around the room to find that I was all alone and I quickly packed up that Gohonzon, and all its sub parts, ran outside, and quickly through it in the trash. That night I repented and asked God to forgive me. I went to work the next morning still shaken by the previous night's audible visitation.

My supervisor and I had become very good friends, and she noticed the change in my attitude. She walked over to my desk and requested my presence in her office. She inquired about my attitude and we sifted through my life's distresses. She knew that I had a relationship with The Lord and suggested that I visit her church. I accepted her offer.

Sunday after Sunday the choir would minister to my brokenness until my position of warming up the pew in the back row, changed to me worshiping alongside the saints and eventually, I joined.

I knew what to do because of my previous experience at the last church so I did not hesitate to talk with the pastor. In a private conversation we talked about my struggle with homosexuality and he expressed that they were a church that "loved everybody" regardless of their background. I told him that he had nothing to fear, for I was not interested in his sheep. I firmly expressed that I only needed him to preach The Word of God and make Jesus real to me again.

Just as quickly as God displayed and demonstrated His love and forgiveness, Satan also decided to show up along with his arsenal and strategy to kill, steal, and destroy.

My supervisor's daughter (will call her Lala) returned from college and we had not seen each other since she left. This Sunday, I chose to sit directly behind her. During service, when it was time to "greet your neighbor," she turned around and was both surprised and overjoyed to see me. We slid each other notes all through service and neither one of us paid attention to the sermon that Sunday. Our friendship was forged, and Jesus had begun to move mightily in my life.

Here goes the set-up: filled with The Holy Spirit and attending a church whose doctrine did not operate in the Gifts of The Spirit, dressing in jeans and sneakers gave much to be desired, and I stuck out like a fat pimple.

Very unfamiliar of the doctrine and protocol (at my previous church I was able to move freely in the power of The Holy Spirit) I was unaware of the attention it brought me. Pastor Mary Parker, who was operating in the office of an Evangelist at that time, was teaching Bible study for our pastor. After class, she walked over to me and said, "Sister, I see the power and anointing of God all over your life."

My thoughts flashed back to the mysterious disappearing woman and I just smiled and said, "Praise The Lord."

I loved to minister The Word of God and on many occasions, I ministered to Lala. Often after Sunday service, I would see her making her way through the crowd to speak to the pastor. In the beginning, I did not make much of it, but it seemed to be a Sunday ritual. They would start to talk and then she would follow him into his office and he would close the door behind them. I began to grow in the knowledge of God, and he was giving me revelation knowledge of His Word. Lala and I would meet in the parking lot after Wednesday night Bible study, and she would listen attentively as I expounded upon The Word and revelation that I received from The Holy Spirit. She and I would be so engrossed in each other's conversation that we never noticed the piercing looks of the other members passing by in their cars.

Not realizing I had the gift of discernment, I had my own "after service meeting" in the pastor's office. It was then that I told him I was aware of his affair with my supervisor's daughter and that he needed to keep that thang in his pants. In his office, he dropped to his knees, and begged me not to expose him to his church. Repeatedly he begged me not to tell her mother.

One late night my phone rang, and I heard the uncontrollable weeping of a woman and as I attempted to calm the caller down, I was able to recognize the voice on the other end. It was Lala. During my intercessory prayer time, The Holy Spirit had already revealed to me what had been going on behind the closed doors of the pastor's office, and this was the call that God had ordained for her to receive her breakthrough. We met privately (I realize now, that this was one of the many traps that the enemy would use to set me up for failure), and she confessed her affair with the pastor and of his attempts to discourage her from being friends with a "dyke." I listened with compassion, and when I heard The Holy Spirit in my heart, I spoke a word to her and guided her through the Word of God where she read that she could be forgiven (1 John 1:9). Before I went to sleep, I went over all the words that her heart poured out that night.

It all confirmed Pastor's sudden dislike of homosexuals after confirming when I first arrived, that his church "welcomed all." The closer Lala and I became, the more his sermons were about gays, hell, and damnation. Let me keep it real. He was not operating in love, compassion or grace. He was operating in his flesh, meaning the gentleness of The Holy Spirit did not lead him. He used the pulpit as a platform to display false righteous indignation, and to mark his territory.

Game recognized game, and his ego was being stepped on because he wanted that little sheep all to himself. That was not the first, nor would it be the last of his indirect (he never inserted my name personally in his sermon) pulpit pot shots.

My mother's illness was in its last stages and she was tired of fighting. COPD is a slow death. She was taking pills to counter act pills, to counter act pills. What she needed was air and the lung capacity to inhale and I had neither to give her. She had suffered for ten years with this disease, in and out of ICUs. Each time the telephone rang, and it was a nurse calling from the emergency room, I would think, "Is this it?" Despite the argumentative nature of our relationship, my mother was my rock and to see her suffer left me feeling utterly hopeless. Although I rehearsed in my mind how to handle funeral arrangements, grieving family members, and the lengthy process of a Catholic burial, the reality of death didn't set in until I received that final phone call.

On January 3, 1991, my mother's doctor called me into a meeting to say he was administering the morphine drip that would slow her heart and cause her to pass away with little or no pain. The doctor had treated my mother for many years and although for most physicians the protocol is not getting emotionally involved with their patients, he shed many tears as he explained the procedure. I had tried to prepare myself for this day, but in that moment, nothing could prepare me for the words her doctor had just spoken. I sat in my mother's hospital room and watched the morphine drip. I could hear the beating of the machines as she struggled for air. Moms was tired, and I could see it in her eyes. She was ready to go.

The Lord used my experience of salvation as the instrument for redemption, and she accepted The Lord Jesus as her savior. I read her favorite scripture out of Psalms 23 and whispered in her ear, "Go home Ma, I'll be okay." On January 4, at 4:30 a.m., my mother took her final breath.

A year had passed since my mother died and on September 13, 1992, Pastor Ross Garrison was the guest speaker at our church. That morning, he spoke a prophetic word into my spirit that changed my life forever. As he delivered the message, I remember physically rocking back and forth in my seat as I held on to every word that fell out of his mouth. When he was finished and began to minister in song, he called me over to his piano and said, "Sister, God has a word for you. He told me to tell you that He is going to deliver you out of the land of your affliction, and not only is He going to deliver you, but also, God is going to use your testimony to bring others out."

Immediately, I thought of all my home girls and wondered, "When? Where? How, God?" The pastor of the church wanted to take the credit for the prophecy, so he called one of his deacons over to bring him some anointing oil and he rubbed it all over my head, pulled me, and together we fell to the floor as he tried to shake the homosexual spirit out of me.

The following Friday night we had another visiting pastor. As a member of the choir, I was in uniform. The choir colors for that night were gold and purple and I did not own any skirts or dresses, so I matched it up with a gold blouse and purple slacks. I had not transitioned into dresses and skirts, but I was coordinated.

Our pastor asked if I would mind giving my testimony and again, The Holy Spirit moved mightily and there was not a dry eye in the house. However, I notice during the testimony that the visiting pastor kept looking me up and down. I remember him leaning over to the pastor and I read his lips. He said, "Is she for real?" The next day during service, our pastor preached about homosexuality as a sin and abomination. On that day, he looked me straight in the eye and began loading his 12-gauge. He openly attacked the authenticity of my testimony and it took me off guard. Repeatedly, he continued his personal assaults; and his words poured out like a flood of glass shards ripping into my flesh.

I sat there horrified and perplexed, not understanding why he was attacking my testimony. I thought, "Jesus did all the things I said He did. Why is God allowing this to happen to me?" I could not believe what I was hearing and seeing.

The pastor whooped, hollered, and vigorously put his hands together as if he was dusting something off, to show by example that this was the motion of two women having sex together. As I heard the roar of laughter and applause echoing in the sanctuary, I just froze and could not move or open my mouth to defend myself. As he fed into the members' applause, he continued his assault by saying, "We can't have women in the church walking around with pants, cutting their hair off and looking like men." I could feel the piercing looks from the congregation. I heard the snickers. I heard the, "Yes Lords" and, "Amen, brother pastor." Even the elder mothers peeped underneath their big hats proclaiming, "That's right, preach!" I sank low into my chair and it felt like he kicked me in my chest. I took every assault. I wanted to defend myself and inside my head, my thoughts were screaming, "Say something!" but I just could not get my body to stand up. All sorts of questions rushed across my mind like, "If he felt this way, why couldn't he talk to me privately?" One of the sisters sitting next to me put her hand on my shoulder and said, "It's ok Sis, he doesn't really mean it."

"Jesus, my friend, my deliverer, my helper, where are you?" I thought. I knew He promised to never leave nor forsake me, but at that moment I felt alone. If I had the strength I would have run, but my body felt like it was riddled with bullets by the pastor's personal and malicious attacks. I sat paralyzed, enduring the pain as I thought about Malcolm X on the day he stood to speak and a hired hit men gunned him down. Finally, I said, "Holy Spirit if you can just give me strength to stand I can run out of this place." He did, and I gathered my things, lifted up my head and pushed past church folk trying to console me and briskly walked towards the exit of the church. The deacons stood at the double doors with arms folded across their chests that gestured I was not to leave. It was like they wanted me to endure the scrutiny, but rage looked back at them and said, "If you don't open this bleep bleeping' door, I'll tear this bleep up."

Some other deacons tried to console me, but their words were ineffective.

The pastor was already outside and I walked up to him with my fists balled up. I looked at him with rage in my eyes and without saying a word, ran across the street to use the phone and called a friend for a ride home.

That night in my apartment, I paced back and forth. I was angry and wanted to whoop that pastors (bleep).

I questioned God in an accusatory tone about His love and protection. I even questioned His existence.

I then swore by Heaven and Earth as a matter of fact; I screamed, "As the angels in heaven are my witness, I will never step foot in another church as long as I live."

Amid my ranting, the telephone rang. It was Evangelist Mary Parker. She tried to comfort me with her words and the only words that I could remember her saying, "Sister Cheryl, I'm so sorry for what happened to you today. Whatever you do, please, don't charge what happen to you today against God."

I respectfully listened, but it fell on death ears and I still questioned God's love for me. I wanted to know why He would allow this to happen.

That night, I decided to cool off and take a long drive and while I drove, I had another conversation. This time it was not with Jesus.

The devil and I talked, as I drove to a spot overlooking the Bay Area.

We chatted, smoked a blunt and drank cognac. Then, the devil said, "Get out of the car; let us reason together, for I wish to show you a thing."

The devil and I stood together at the top of the hill.

I listened intently as he said, "I know your struggle and I feel your pain of displacement. You are not what church or society would define as feminine, nor can your anatomy define you as a man. But, I accept you just the way you are, and I could give you a nation where you can rule, a nation where a woman can be a king."

Suddenly, it appeared as if the whole Bay Area lit up and I could see lights glimmering and sparkling before my eyes as I beheld my new kingdom.

Subtlety, he put a crown on my head, a purple robe around my shoulders, and placed a scepter in my hand to rule.

Satan whispered in my ear, "If you bow down and worship me, I will give you all this territory, gold and fame."

Through the hazy eyes of cognac, the effects on my mind from the weed, and painful memories, I accepted the devil's offer and returned to what I knew best, women, money, dope and the hustle.

It was 10 years before I stepped into another church.

With the painful loss of my mother and all that had transpired in my life, it brought Lala and I closer together.

We dated for a few years and for the first time in my lesbian experience, I took it to another level and asked her to marry me.

Everybody boasted about our beautiful summer union with over 200 family and friends in attendance.

I can recall walking down the aisle on my special day and The Holy Spirit whispering in my ear saying, "This is not of me."

How right He was for in three months, and $8,000 later, our union was annulled.

According to Satan's plan, things were beginning to line up.

I had gone back to where I started, and my life had come full circle.

CHAPTER 7: SATAN'S COVENANT MANIFESTS

In December of 1995, I passed the California State Barber's exam. Next, I spent two years working under a Master Barber. Then in 1997 I opened my first barber shop called, 'Fades 4 Ya' and my confidence and popularity was restored.

I was so full of pride and the devil was starting to fulfill his covenant with me.

Gifted as a barber, I groomed men often better than most of the brothas in Sacramento. Clients poured in from everywhere. My money was long, and my pockets stayed fat. I rented a luxury two-bedroom apartment overlooking a lake and furnished it with all the bachelor swag including an 8-foot red velvet slate pool table that was centered in the living room.
In the upper corners, I mounted two 25-inch television monitors showing the hottest stripper videos. My alpine home had surround sound bumpin' hip-hop rhythms all through the apartment and the homies stopped by often to shoot dice, and slam bones. We drank until we passed out from the bar I had stocked with top shelf liquor.

I had posters of the hottest top models on the walls. I converted the spare bedroom into a smoking lounge.

There were always women in the kitchen cooking for me and naked women stretched out in front of roaring fireplace.

I was truly living the life of a player, and I dated the most beautiful women. I was single, financially stable, and I drove a 528 BMW. However, with all the material wealth I gained, internally, my soul had no peace.

I became involved again in the "Isms" of spiritual things, including the New Age Movement. I created my destiny by using creative visualization. To me, life had become a blank canvas and every day I had the power within myself (and with help from my covenant partner, Satan) to paint whatever picture I chose.

With all the material possessions and a bounty of beautiful women, there was a deep pain I could not cover up, and a spiritual void I could not fill. It seemed that whatever I tried to do, I could not silence the small voice that had continued to call, drawing me to read God's Word. Every time I thought about reading The Bible, the image of that terrible day reminded me of why I would not.

With pain, anger, and bitterness rising inside me, I used every chance I had to manipulate God's word. I studied everything about the origin of Christianity and debated the authenticity of the King James Version and over time, I could manipulate and twist The Word of God to sway others away from the faith and toward my selfish doctrine.

As I continued to live my life, I remember meeting a woman at a New Year's Goal-Setting Party; she was not a Sacramento resident but had moved here from the south. She was a gorgeous woman with cocoa brown skin and a big, beautiful smile. This cocoa brown honey was a single parent who found my conversation intriguing. Quite comfortable in my presence, she stated that she didn't trip about homosexuals and affirmed to me often in our many conversations that she was waiting for her king. When she told me about her ménage a trois experience (that involved another woman), I was quick to affirm that she could never know true pleasure from a one-night stand, or the comfort and security a woman could give another woman in a relationship. This southern sister, raised to believe that homosexuality was a sin, was confronted with metaphysic manipulation. Quickly I twisted The Word of God and echoed Satan's words that he whispered in Eve's ear in the Garden of Eden saying, "Did God really say that?" (Genesis 3:1)

Recognizing her brokenness, I took advantage of her loneliness and conspiratorially whispered that her inquisitiveness was going to lead her to experience lesbianism. She emotionally fought the urge; however, her intrigue gave her away.

It was a challenge to bait her and I loved challenges. I was the hunter and my persuasive strategy worked like this; once I got a woman interested, I would draw back and reverse the game so that the hunter became the hunted. This was my world and I had the advantage. I knew how to play the game and I always played to win. My assignment was always to conquer and capture. The more this woman resisted and argued that she would never become involved with a woman, the more I pulled her in with images of sexual passion and words filled with lusty overtones.

Calmly and with gentleness, I relentlessly planted new deliciously sinful thoughts.

Months later, I hosted a small party and purposely invited one of my single stud partners. Like fruit on the vine, I knew my new "Southern Sexy" was ripe for the picking.

At the party, I introduced them and within a month's time, she forgot all about her "King" and enjoyed the pleasures of a woman's company. Just that quick, she was "turned out" and her identity in was in question. This was always the end of the story with most straight women. The game never changes, only the players.

I began to love whom I had become. I was posing as the light but, I had become Satan's ambassador. The words of heterosexual women, trying to resist the lure was the fuel that drove my passion and it was like the smell of blood to the hungry lion.

I met many women like her, always with the predictable ending. Curious straight women always proclaiming things like, "Can't no woman satisfy me like a man." They would also say, "Cheryl, that ain't my cup of tea" or "I don't play on that side of the tracks." Then, there was the all-time famous straight girl line. They would say, "Cheryl, I don't know what it is about you, I'm not gay and I'm not attracted to women, but I feel so comfortable around you." As a skillful hunter, the take down was what I lived for.

When I had them cuddled tightly together under the warm sheets, and hearing her sighs of satisfaction, I would just lie there with a pompous grin, chuckle and say, "Another one bites the dust."

CHAPTER 8: THE FALLEN SOLDIER

My father's heroin addiction came to a screeching halt and because of his continued drug use; he suffered a brain aneurysm and stroke.

Now I was angrier, especially since our relationship grew closer after the death of my mother and he said he was getting help for his addiction. His stroke situation obviously revealed his lie. It had taken us four years to heal and him gain my trust and then this happened.

After his recovery, I went to visit and sat on the edge of his bed and we began to talk when suddenly, his eyes were filled with tears. He removed his oxygen mask and said, "Baby, Ddaddy is sorry for the pain I caused both you and your mother. I am sorry that I was not there for you. Can you find it in your heart to forgive me?" I had longed to hear those words from my dad and as the tears rolled down my face, I answered, "Yes, daddy, I forgive you. I love you."

On October 4, 2002, a nurse from the Veteran's Hospital telephoned and said I needed to get to the hospital. I walked to my father's room, opened the blinds so that he could see the sunny Sacramento day. In that moment, again, the still small voice rescued my pain from that terrible day, and as I experienced with my mother, I sat on the edge of his bed and began to read the 23rd Psalm.

I said, "Daddy, just open your eyes for me, just one last time." Somehow, wherever headed, he turned around to say goodbye because he opened his eyes for the final time. My dad looked directly at me as one single tear rolled down his cheek and again I felt a familiar presence of peace.
It was all over the room. I could not explain it. I bent down and whispered in his ear, "Tell mom I love her. You can go home now; I am going to be fine. I am in The Lord's hands."

Certainly, this was an absolute contradiction to my lifestyle at the time. I do not know why I said that in that way, but by 8:30 a.m., my father took his final breath. He was the only man I trusted and loved. He was my hero and fallen soldier

CHAPTER 9: NO WHERE TO HIDE

One of the brothers whom I befriended at the church where the assassination occurred, whom also was victimized by homosexual bashing for ministering in song with a towel, found a new church home.
For years, this brother would invite me to his church and as an anointed psalmist, he would continually drop off Gospel CDs and sermon messages. He would faithfully recline in my barber chair to receive his bi-weekly grooming.

I would wait and almost purposefully bait him in a debate about The Word of God. I had gotten so good at it that I would often bring him to silence. (He was listening and waiting for the leading of The Holy Spirit to minister.) I was relentless in attacking his faith, but this was a different type of day and as part of our normal bi-weekly routine, he talked about his pastor's love for the un-loveable, his new church family, and of course, The Word of God.

Like always, I countered with my New Age philosophy. When his haircut was finished, he rose from the chair. I watched this brother's frame heighten from six feet tall to what appeared to be nine feet. Quickly, he turned towards me. With conviction and authority, he looked me dead in my eyes, pointed his prophetic finger in my face, and said, "Cheryl, you have a powerful anointing on your life. You know Jesus is your Lord and Savior, but more importantly I want you to know, Jesus knows who you are, and I don't care what you say, or what you've read, you can't hide!"

I tried a witty retort, but the words got caught in my throat. I remembered somewhere in The Bible where it said, "For The Word of God is quick, and powerful, and sharper than any two-edged sword, piercing even to the dividing asunder of soul and spirit, and of the joints and marrow, and is a discerner of the thoughts and intents of the heart" (Hebrews 4:12).

After that encounter, I found myself reading The Bible more and I opened a small window into my "inner man" and agreed to visit this brother's church.

A few days before rolling into his church, I assumed my most masculine position, looked into his compassionate eyes and rebelliously made this statement, "I'm wearing my jeans and sneakers, and I'm bringing my girl." He smiled and said, "Just come as you are, I've told my pastor all about you." I thought, here we go again, I'm going to walk in with my girl and the pastor is going to change his sermon from a "God is Love Series" to "Homosexuality and abomination." Much to my surprise however, the pastor stood before God's people and spoke about a man named Jesus and His love for all people.

As Pastor spoke, I sat calmly in my chair, attentively listening in amazement to the grace and love of Jesus Christ.

I began to attend regularly and each Sunday my heart was being restored. One Sunday after another awesome service, the invitation to Christ was offered. I looked at my partner with a "you know what I'm about to do" look and made my way down to the altar and rededicated my life to Christ.

Sunday after Sunday, Pastor would preach Jesus's love and healing grace and during these sermons, I could feel The Holy Spirit performing open-heart surgery and restoring my faith.

One night after a New Membership Class, I spoke with Pastor confidentially and said, "Stop making me cry in church, I'm a pimp." We laughed and hugged. As he walked away to greet and speak with other members, I remember sensing a divine connection with this man. He saw and pulled things out of me that no one did. I knew that a bond of love was developing between us. His church had become for me, a house of refuge, restoration and release.

I looked forward to each New Membership Class, Bible Study and Sunday service. I asked a thousand questions and he answered them one by one. After he gave me his cell phone number, I called him so often; I had my own ring tone. I grew to love my new shepherd. The reality was that next to my father, he was the only other man I ever loved.

He showed loved to everyone that attended. He loved the homosexuals, adulterers, liars, gossipers, and dope addicts. He once told me that he had asked God to send him all the people that other churches did not want. Well, there I was, and his ministry looked like the island of misfit toys.

We did eventually have the discussion on homosexuality and his response was, "I don't condone it Cheryl, and I don't have the power to change you. The Word of God will do that. I'm here to be your shepherd and lead you to Jesus Christ. It is The Word of God that has the life-changing power, not me." He went on to say, "I see a powerful anointing on your life and God revealed to me, who you are to him. It is up to you to trust God. Stay on the front line and never let the enemy know the length of your sword."

On December 24, 2003, I purchased a ring, and I proposed to the woman I had been dating. My plan was to register us as domestic partners, buy a home, have her artificially inseminated and live a "normal" lesbian life. Life was good, or so I thought.

To explain what was to take place in the next six months is difficult, but I will try to the best of my ability.

The healing that was taking place and the longing to be in the presence of God was overwhelming. The more I read The Scriptures, the closer and more personal Jesus became. My nights were often interrupted with visions of standing before thousands of people and preaching God's Word. Always, the still small voice constantly calling to me. Finally, one night I answered, "Yes, Lord," and fell prostrate on the floor and began to weep. I just know that I was tired of persecuting His Holy Word. I knew that His Word was Life.

Often my partner would find me in the middle of the night at the kitchen table studying The Scriptures. My desire for physical intimacy was waning and my desire to feed my spirit was increasing. I knew that our relationship was ending. I kept pressing to draw closer to The Lord through His Word, and The Holy Spirit was engrafting my spirit into the heart of God.

I discussed this change with by best friend, Mrs. Williams. Mrs. Williams is a short elderly woman of wisdom well past retirement age, but still working part-time, not for the money, but the opportunity to use the wisdom of God to teach His love for all people. We became friends while working together for a health care company and found that we had mutual friends. Since meeting her, she has become my spiritual mother, confidant and counselor. We talk about everything, including every woman and experience as a lesbian.

When it was time to introduce my new woman to "moms", she would later say to me, "Baby, she's not the one." It was as if she had this inside track on my destiny because she would say, "Cheryl, you will always repeat the test, until you pass it." She was always right as I would be filled with excitement over my new love and in less than three years, the relationship would end and I would be leading the single life again.

I took the role of the stud (man) in each relationship and as a result, each time there was a breakup, I lost all my material possessions and had to start over purchasing furniture, electronics, silverware, etc.

I was being torn in two directions—trying to draw closer to God, but still trying to hold on to my lesbian orientation. It hurt to see the pain in my partner's eyes, but how could she fight against God and what He was doing in my life?

CHAPTER 10: THE REVELATION AND RELEASE

I struggled internally with the question that if Jesus was love, and God had given us freewill, what kind of gift is free when the love of another woman brings condemnation and eternal damnation according to scripture.

I paced at night, prayed and was becoming frustrated because I believed that once I had drawn near to God I would hear from Him. I wanted answers, and I needed now.

One evening while sitting at my kitchen table with some members of church, we began to talk about our ministry, church vision, and the personal struggles that we were all dealing with. I brought up the fact that I still did not have a complete conviction about being a lesbian. After each one had their demeaning retorts backed with scriptural references, I turned up a 40-ounce bottle of Mickey's malt liquor to my lips. I guzzled 8-10 ounces, slammed the bottle down on the table and yelled, "I don't want Paul, Matthew, Mark, Luke, John or your Pastor giving me their opinions about it. Jesus himself has to tell me that homosexuality is a sin.
Jesus rose from the dead, gave sight to the blind, and His Father parted the Red Sea." I said, "Surely changing me should be a small thing for such a big God."

I hit another nerve because my brother with the same prophetic finger stood up and said, "Little Saul, you are about to have a Damascus experience!"

As I left for work the following morning, my mind filled with thoughts of homosexual relationships with women, I pondered, is it really a sin? When I got to the barbershop, I sat in my barber's chair and opened my Bible. I troubled along the pages until I stopped on the 8th Chapter of the book of John. It was about a woman taken in adultery. The worship CD playing set the atmosphere in the shop. Suddenly, the CD stopped.

I felt the silence of the shop as I continued to read. As I read, I felt my body transport back in time. I saw every pastor, every holly roller, every anti-gay activist and all who believed that homosexuality was a sin, standing behind me. The story continues, when they put her in front of the crowd, they begin their case proclaiming, "Lord, this woman was caught in the very act of homosexuality. The Law of Moses says to stone her. What do you say?"

Jesus stooped down and sat next to me. They kept demanding an answer, so He stood up and said, "All right, stone her, but, let those who have never sinned throw the first stones!" Then He stooped down again and sat next to me, this time even closer. When the accusers heard this, one by one, they dropped their stones, turned, and walked away. The scene faded to black. Jesus and I were alone in the silence of the barbershop. Then Jesus stood up again and said, "Where are your accusers? Is there anyone left to condemn you?" "No, Lord." I said. Then Jesus said, "Neither do I condemn thee. Go and sin no more." Suddenly I felt His glory fill the barbershop and my life; destiny and purpose all became clear, including the answer to my question. Jesus, I now understood, carried every one of my afflictions, all my sin, so that I could be free.

I knew with a certainty that Jesus loved me and would always be with me. The point that I could not see through the lenses of pain was Jesus as a God of holiness, a God of righteousness and his grace forgave me.

I did not deserve it. I could not earn it. His love is a gift, and gifts are FREE! Suddenly, I could hear the judge's mallet; it swung down and declared "NOT GUILTY." When the Word of God said Jesus stooped down, I saw Him stooping down in front of me. Jesus got right in the center of my circumstance and met me where I was. I interpreted this experience as my, "God encounter" or in my brother's case, my "Damascus experience." The Bible never describes this woman's features or gives an in-depth description of her past life. However, what was important in my situation, Jesus saw past my circumstance and met my need, just where I was. The words, "Go and sin no more," echoed in the barbershop and penetrated my heart and soul. It hit me harder than all the words from the pastor on that terrible day. The revelation illuminated in my spirit and the revelation became clear. Jesus always loved me. He just hates sin. It did not matter who it was or who was doing it. Fornication outside of marriage; the marriage God ordained, is a sin.

I spent the remaining week in intense prayer. I never touched my partner sexually again.

It was now June, and months had passed since my barbershop experience and during a Minister's Training class, I stood up and shouted, "Pastor, I can't run, I can't hide, I can't sleep, I've been called to preach The Gospel, and I submit to the will of The Lord for my life and ministry."
The other students began to shout and cry. He stretched out his arms and I ran into them, almost knocking us both over.

Without knowing what was to happen next, Sunday morning came and the church was filled with praise and the spirit of worship. Little did I know that God was still completing the work He had begun in the barber shop.

A minister from Berkeley California was visiting that Sunday and I never knew that God would use her as His instrument and mighty vessel of deliverance. Her large frame slowly approached me, and I could hear her purpose in her walk. Her feet sounded like thunder in my ears. She walked up beside me and said, "Sister, The Lord asked me to come and pray with you." A little leery from my earlier church experiences, including the dousing of my head with oil and tackling me to the ground, I submitted to her invitation to pray for me. I lifted my hands and she placed her hand upon my stomach and said, "In the name of Jesus, I command you spirit of perversion to loose this woman in the name of Jesus." I fell forward and from the deepest part of my vocal chords, I screamed. I could hear my prophetic brother rejoicing as he said, "That thing is coming out of her."

The church fell silent and I could feel myself trying to catch my breath.
As I began to clear my eyes and focus on my surroundings, I felt the saints
lifting me off the floor. I did not remember falling. I was weak-kneed and
wobbly, feeling one hundred pounds lighter as they lifted me up.

When I looked for the Pastor, he was shaking his head as if in amazement
at The Holy Spirit's awesome power.

That same afternoon, after service, I climbed the stairs to our apartment
and opened the door slowly, entering the room where my partner sat.
The look in her eyes and the expression on her face confirmed to me that
she was prepared for what I was about to say. I told her that I loved her
very much and that I apologize for anything that I have done to hurt her.
I asked for her forgiveness and went on to tell her that I had acknowledged
my calling as a minister of The Gospel. I shared with her the experience
during our morning service and that God had set me free.

We both understood, I could no longer continue with our relationship.
The rest of that afternoon until the rising of the sun, we held each other.
We talked, cried, and before she left for work, we declared God's peace
and blessing for each other's lives.

CHAPTER 11: WHEN GOD DID NOT ANSWER

By July, I had moved out and into my own apartment. I spent the first few weeks in tears. I had difficulty unpacking, and many boxes remained unopened on the kitchen floor. I felt alone and isolated.
I felt like the walls were closing in on me. I prayed and cried out to The Lord, but He did not answer. As months passed, I began to come under a fierce spiritual attack. I would see shadows and one night a demonic entity sat on my chest. I rebuked it, and it disappeared (Nahum 1:4).

Most of my friends had heard of my conversion, so there were not many telephone calls. The life I once knew was no longer an option, and the life God had planned for me seemed un-doable. The apartment never really had the warmth or characteristics of a home and nothing about it resembled anything that was part of my former life. It was cold, and I felt like I was starting to lose my mind. I spent several nights sleeping outside in my truck because it was the only place familiar to me.

I continued to attend church and I tried to keep a cheerful countenance to hide my pain. Night after night, I paced in my empty apartment, praying and waiting for God to speak. I don't know what I was expecting Him to say; I just needed to hear His encouraging word. I felt like I was hovering in space, suspended in a celestial dream. There was no one to talk to or share this suffering.

I learned quickly that people could feel for you from a perspective of human love and compassion. But unless they have gone through and experienced what you have experienced, they cannot understand the depth of the pain I felt.

I found a Christian group of ex-homosexuals that met on Thursday nights, but I couldn't really connect, because everyone seemed to have had a legitimate reason for choosing to live the lifestyle. Rape, molestation, physical abuse, rejection, environment, abandonment; break-ups gone wild, baby daddy impregnating the BFF, or a generation of lesbians in the family, etc.; these were the case(s) of many of them.

After listening to their stories, I found I did not fall into any of these categories.
I tried to talk it over with my pastor, but the look in his eyes, said, "I don't have a clue. This is a road I never traveled." Faithfully, he encouraged me to "stay on the battlefield." He said, "Don't give up your position in Christ regardless of what your circumstances look like." His words were comforting, but they could not fill the empty void I felt.

The pain of transformation flowed deep inside my sou. It was feeling like my flesh was separating from my bones. I cried out, "Where are you God, I need to feel your presence?" Once you have experienced a "God encounter," you will never forget it. Your soul will continually thirst for it. Running through my mind, were thoughts like, "I did everything you asked. I had repented, I had submitted, I broke off my engagement.
I'm sharing The Gospel with everyone I can. I'm practicing celibacy. Lord, I do not know this place and I can't hear your voice anymore!
Where are you Jesus! Is this a test? Are you listening? Can you feel my pain?"

Hopelessness hovered over me, and I remembered the fifth of Remy Martin and some old marijuana on top of the frig. So I sat down and prepared my escape from the pain.

Hours passed, so did that fifth and the fat sativa blunt.

Again, Jesus got jokes cuz with all that was in my system, I was not high.
I thought to myself, "Great, God, you won't even let me get high."

Strangely, I dried my eyes and remembered a tin box with pictures of all my ex-girlfriends in it. I laid each picture out according to the times, and history of the relationships. I looked deeply into the faces of each of them. I saw different shades of skin, race, hair colors and styles; their eyes and smiles were each different, but there was something common about all of them. I would later discover the thread that bound these women together.

Before I went off the deep end, I terminated my lease and rented a room from the music director at church. Let me pause here for a moment: Frank Fanner, I will always love you brother. Thank you for rescuing me. When I moved into my new room, I was instantly at peace.
I found a secret place. My burdens lifted, and the pressures of owning a business, separation from my partner, and other uncertainties seemed like a distant past. My prayer life was back on track and The Holy Spirit began to repair my broken vessel.

The Holy Spirit poured into me. Wisdom and knowledge of His plan for my life became clear.

As I laid in my bed, feeling rest at last, my only thought was of all those women and what they had in common.

CHAPTER 12: THE DAMASCUS EXPEREINCE

I recall being asked by the First Lady of the church to preach my initial first sermon on Women's Missionary Sunday. I was honored that she allowed me to grace the pulpit. Likewise, I was on fire for God and He had given me a Word for His people.

That night, before I preached, I relaxed in the presence of wise counsel.
My spiritual mother and I talked about my ministry, life's journeys, and the delicious Chinese food we were eating. As always, she spoke with melodic poetry filled with wisdom for the soul. I talked about all my ex- girlfriends, and I told her the one thing I recognized, they were heterosexual, and experienced some type of brokenness. Not one woman was gay. I asked her why I attracted broken, straight women, and was I some sort of "straight girl magnet?" "Daughter" she said, The Lord will answer.

Not long after dinner, I left the house and while driving, I shouted, "Why Lord?" He responded that night, audibly, just as if I heard Him, as I sat in front of that Gohonzon in my apartment that night some years before. The Holy Spirit's voice said, "Daughter, the women that you attracted, were drawn to what was inside of you. They saw the light in you from the dark places of their life." I answered, "But, I loved them, I truly cared, and wanted to heal their pain." He said, "I know but I love them more. You are the light but I am the LIGHTHOUSE. You weren't supposed to have sex with them, you were supposed to minister to them, and for this purpose, have I called you out of the land of your affliction."
I pulled the truck over and my whole life and lifestyle passed before me.
Suddenly, I knew the commonality of all of them.

Then, I was reminded of a conversation my ex and I shared. She said, "Cheryl, I don't have experience in this lifestyle and I don't want to be hurt. Please protect my heart." It began to roll like a movie, Face after face, their story played.

Making it home, I fell on the floor of my room and wept uncontrollably. Like Jacob, I wrestled with God for which seemed like eternity declaring, "I refuse to let you go until you tell me who I am. What is my name? What felt like a flood of water released from the Nimbus dam, I laid motionless as the still small voice whispered His reply, and I heard, "WOMAN."

Sitting on top of a stack of books and my eyes filled with tears, I looked up and read the VHS tape that my cousin Aaron had given me titled "Identity Theft." Suddenly, the revelation came. MY IDENTITY WAS STOLEN, and because the enemy had stolen my identity, He used me to steal the identities of other women. I needed to compose myself, so I began to pray.

As I asked for God's forgiveness the telephone rang. It was 12:45 a.m. and it was my ex-partner. She heard that I was preaching my first sermon and called to congratulate me. I shared with her the revelation that God had given me that night, I apologized, and she forgave me.

I began to give God praise and now I understand being more seasoned and mature that God did not abandon me. When I looked back over my life, I realized, God's amazing grace sustained me.

It was now 20 years after I responded to an altar call, and I was to preach my first sermon. God sustained me.

That Sunday nine people gave their life to Christ that day.

I once stood in bondage. Now, I am broken and free.

CHAPTER 13: NAKED AND NOT ASHAMED

Hello Reader!
I am so glad that you decided to continue with me. This process has not been an easy journey, or an easy book to write. The warfare, even as I revised this book has been heavy. I broke out with bumps all over my back. The laptop I used to finish this book, the "H" and "B" keys continued to stick.

A very close clergy friend sat in my chair and said, "Did God really say write the book?" Their question brought doubt to my mind during the process.

OMG! I can go on and on about what I went through with this book, but I must stress this point. I do not, I repeat, I DO NOT, believe in superstition or coincidence.

This book did not just find you by accident. I believe in the divine order and appointed time of Gods perfect will.

Whether you are straight, gay, a parent, or in ministry, God placed this book in your hands-on purpose. So, give yourself a break and keep reading.

I do not have any 12 or 6-Step process on how to overcome homosexuality. I took one-step to Jesus, and He still walks with me today. Jesus was patient in my deliverance, so I will patiently walk with you regarding your decision.

Homosexuality is a very sensitive subject for those struggling with their identities and trying to find hope in God.

I believe that the information in this book, I pray, will also aid and assist Christian leadership who need to address or counsel this community if or when they become partners with their church. Lord knows people in the community have listened to enough gay bashing, hell's flames, and abomination messages that left them with no hope—and no Jesus.

Sinners come into the house of God, desperately searching for hope for their situations. Some homosexuals are coming out of occults, generational curses, addiction; emotionally and physically abusive relationships; abandonment, and rejection. And like many heterosexual's, they too are broken, beaten and weary from life's prejudices and the world's assaults. They look to the church for refuge, so why preach sermons that close the door to their final outreach of hope. Why pour salt on open wounds and not give light to salvation's path? That is like a pastor recognizing a crack addict in his congregation and preaching a sermon about how crack kills and about how addicted parents put their children in the crossfire for a blast. They whoop and jump up and down saying, "Throw away your crack pipes and Gerber jars and find Jesus." Sorry folks, it just doesn't work like that.

My deliverance from homosexuality directly came from the love and grace of Jesus Christ. Grace, beloved, enables us to conquer, overcome, and have victory in every area of our lives. His love reaches to the lowest gutters of our lives, shines light in the darkness, and brings us to safety.

Jesus is a loving, long-suffering, patient, forgiving and loving savior.
It's His desire, that ALL BE SAVED (John 3:16-17). Jesus came to reclaim His lost sheep (Luke 19:10).

Let me say this with conviction and authority. God's Word transformed me (Romans 12:2). The more of His Word I sowed into my life, the more I began to transform. I did not transform into the image of a run way model or the First Lady of our church. Many believe the evidence of deliverance is an outer manifestation of dresses, make-up, stilettos, and flat irons. I gave the church all of this and it did NOT arrest my desire for women.

Hello!
Relax; salvation does not rest in a dress or a suit. For example, I know of several Christian leaders of mega churches who wore tailored suits, gators, and continued indulging in same sex relationships.

Hello!

Reader, I want you to know and understand that I did not rush out and purchase three-inch stilettoes or spend hundreds of dollars on women's clothing or begin to date men. I do not believe that any of these things authenticated my deliverance. My deliverance began when I repented of my sins (and there were many) and walked in obedience to God's Word. The more I read God's holy word, the more my faith grew in the identity of Christ. I started to believe that I was a new creature in Christ Jesus and that old things were passing away (2 Corinthians 5:17).

Please, comprehend this truth reader and walk with me on this subject. Deliverance (salvation) must first take place within your heart (Romans 10:9)! What I'm saying is that at one time, all of us were an ex-something and our sin separated us from God (Isaiah 59:2). I believe Jesus is more concerned about or souls than our clothes.

Hello!
Holiness is a lifestyle that comes by way of a relationship with a Holy God. A relationship is a commitment of love between two people and when nurtured, the relationship develops into an un-breakable bond.

In my relationship with Him, I began to fall in love with Jesus. I learned to take the same passion that I had with women and redirect it towards My Lord and Savior, Jesus Christ.

Allow me to keep it real; the more quality time I spent with women, the more I desired to please them. I want you to catch this: The more quality time I spend with Jesus, the more I fall in love with Him. The more I begin to fall in love with Him, the more I reverence Him. The more I reverence Him, the more I honor Him. The more I honor Him, the more I desire to be in His presence.

I'm a living witness that nobody who stays in God's presence has ever remained the same.

CHAPTER 14: THE GARDEN

Many books are written on the origin and nature of sin. However, I'm revealing my testimony, from the perspective of my deliverance from homosexuality.

I know, there's some heavy hitters that will challenge my testimony and its authenticity, so let me clarify it now. I am not a scholar, biologist, sociologist, psychologists or theologian. I have no degrees in any of these fields of study; however, I do have a Ph.D in "Lifeology," a master's degree in "Sin" and a BA in "Hard Knocks." So ladies and gentlemen, please get into your starting positions, it's about to go down.

The Holy Spirit led me to Genesis as the foundation for understanding God's relationship with man. I've always considered the Garden of Eden to be the opening curtain for the most phenomenal love story ever told. I'm always fascinated by the romance and awesomeness of God's love for His creation. He serenaded man and lavishly draped him in His glory and coagulated the atmosphere for His divine courtship.

One of my favorite lines is in Genesis 3:8. It reads, "And they (Adam and Eve) heard the voice of The Lord walking in the Garden in the cool of the day." Imagine that! What an honor and privilege to have had this kind of fellowship with The Lord, but how could they forfeit it all for a bite of forbidden fruit (Genesis 2:17)?

To describe God would be another book entirely and to define Him as being one thing would mean to box Him in it. I understand God to be Holy, sovereign, omni-present, infinite, and spirit (and so much more). I agree with the Holman Bible dictionary's commentary that says, "Perhaps the closest we can come to a definition of God is that God is the Holy Being who comes in servant form."

The beginning chapters of Genesis describes the grandeur of God and His love for His Creation. It goes on to describe the creation of man (Genesis 2:7).

What God revealed to me is a transfer of power and authority of what I've come to call, God's spiritual DNA. This impartation of spiritual DNA is what distinguishes us from the rest of creation. The Bible says we are His workmanship, created in His image, set apart for His glory (Ephesians 2:10). Man is not God per se, but created to reflect His character and glory.

Sin originated in the Heavenly realm. Lucifer (Satan) was once one of God's beloved and beautiful angels. I'll go as far as to say that He oversaw the Heavenly choir and was the lead singer of the praise and worship team.

Heaven or "Heavenly Realm" is the place where the presence of The Lord dwells. Eden was a kind of Heaven on Earth. Eden was a consecrated place where The Lord communicated with man. Lucifer, jealous of God and all the worship He received from all that He created, started to believe in his own press and became prideful.

Pride begins in the heart, and out of the abundance of the heart, the mouth speaks (Mathew 12:34). Pride got Satan kicked out of God's grace in Heaven (Isaiah 14:12-14). Pride means and excessively high opinion of oneself; to indulge in self-esteem and glory. In other words, Lucifer one day declared and purposed in his heart to exalt his ministry above God and become like God.

This became funny to me on the back end of things because I thought, "How could this cat truly believe that he had the ability to exalt himself or enlarge his capacity to exceed that of his creator?"

Pride ladies and gentlemen will always seek self-glory and Lucifer (Satan) will always seek to promote his own kingdom agenda.

Next, The Lord God opened my eyes and I received the revelation of the two trees in the Garden of Eden. In Genesis 2:9 God talks about the tree of life and the tree of the knowledge of good and evil. The trees represented choice. I call it "free will choice." The grace of God even extended to man through the explanation of the consequences of eating from the tree (Genesis 2:16-17). I paid special attention to two verses - 16 and 17. The words "command" and "shalt" (shall) stood out to me. Command means to direct with authority, give orders, or instruction. The word shall is defined as determination or promise. In legal terms, shall means that it will come to pass. From this illustration, The Lord God wanted His creation to love Him from a willing heart.

I learned from this that God doesn't force you into loving Him. He desires to share an eternal relationship with man.

In Deuteronomy 30:19, God says, "I call Heaven and Earth to record this day against you, that I have set before you life and death, blessing and cursing; therefore, choose life that both you and thy seed may live."

Predicated on our beliefs, and how we understand life and ourselves, choices can be difficult to make. Always, the choices we make, will determine our consequences, good or bad.

In writing this book, The Holy Spirit reminded me of many unexpected and hazardous courses that the journey of my life took me on. When I came upon certain dead-ends or forks in the road, it would feel as if my thoughts were under arrest, and I was standing in the center of time, and uncertain of whether to choose life or death. Have you ever felt like that?

Hear me now, the reason you are still reading, is God is calling you to Himself, and wants to bring you back to an Eden relationship. Satan's is furious that his relationship with God is cut off. It will NEVER BE LIKE IT WAS, and he is mad about it. Like a scavenger crow, he forever hovers over your life to snatch the seeds (word of faith) from the ground of your heart, never wanting your relationship with God to grow. Remember the old saying, "misery loves company?" Well, Satan is a playa hater.

Therefore, the end of the Garden story goes like this. (I'm paraphrasing.)

Eve, deceived by Satan's cunning tactics of deception, gave Adam a bite of the forbidden fruit and they disobeyed God's commandment by eating the fruit. They forfeited their inheritance of eternal life and were kicked out of the garden. Adam and Eve's disobedience resulted in the birth of sin on earth and so as the offspring of Adam and Eve we are born into a sinful nature (Psalms 51:5 and Romans 5:12).

One might think, this is the conclusion to a sad love story. Ha! Ha! God prevails. Just when it looks like Satan has fulfilled his mission, and just when the outlook for Adam and Eve seemed desperately hopeless, there is the sound of a mighty trumpet in Heaven. Jesus has made a way of escape. Hallelujah! The Garden was always a part of the plan of salvation. He loves us so much, that He knew we would fall so He secured our souls by putting us on layaway (Romans 8:29). He sent His only begotten Son, Jesus Christ, to pay sin's debt. The Word says, "Yet while we were sinners, Christ died for us" (Romans 5:8). Jesus conquered death, Hell and the grave and destroyed the works of the devil (1 John 3:8).

In a relationship with God, He never wants to be separated from you.
He's solid, faithful, and 100% dependable.

As Kendrick Lamar would say, Loyalty. Loyalty. Loyalty.

Now that's what I call a love story.

CHAPTER 15: SATAN'S LEAGAL ACCESS

On many occasions I have said, "This is it! I'm cool on women. I'll just be celibate and live a single life." This idea would last for a while, but I would soon find myself sitting in a bar having deep conversation with a straight female. We would exchange phone numbers and later in that week, we would enjoy the comforts and pleasures of each other's company. Early in morning, I would be climbing out of her bed, putting on my clothes, and trying to find my sneakers.

Several times, I asked The Lord, "Why can't I stay saved. Why can't I shake these feelings for women?" One day, the answer came when The Lord directed me again in the book of Genesis. It was the portion of scripture when Satan tempted and deceived Eve. In the moment, she willfully took a bite of the fruit, and her free will choice resulted in forfeiting her inheritance.

You see beloved, Satan creates the deceptive stage while strategically arranging the people and places in your life to set you up to fall and fail.
Satan can only present the temptation. Even though he can package it specifically to your liking, he cannot force your hand. In simple terms, he can lead you to the water, but legally, he can't make you drink. Satan moves in the realm of legalities. One of the tactics he uses to gain entrance into your life is through your legal authorization; an invite. Here is something to ponder. Let's say you have a spiritual pin number and hidden away in your bank vault are your most valued treasures. Don't you want to protect your most valuable treasures with your life? Satan gains access to your account by your willful authorization, meaning you gave him your pin number.

From a willing heart you choose to be obedient to God and by obeying God's word, you stay in His will, and in the circle of His protection.

When you accepted Jesus Christ as your Lord and savior, (born again) He granted you access to an Inheritance (John 3:3). You become a new citizen (Ephesians 2:19). Now, you legally belong to a country and have the rights, protection, and privileges of that country. The Bible states that you become a joint heir with Jesus (Romans 8:16-17).

I attended a spiritual authority class taught by Pastor Andrea Allen regarding the meaning of the word "Trespass" and I would like to share this information with you. She taught from the book of Ephesians 2:1 and she broke down the first sentence, "...who were dead in trespasses." She said that trespass meant to enter onto another's land illegally. The Greek word for trespass is "Paraptoma" that means to deviate from one's natural course. Now, allow me to break it down for you as Jesus broke it down for me and bring it to this century and subject.

First let me reiterate and emphasize what I mean when I say, "God's circle of protection." This means your life is operating in obedience to The Word of God and not out of your flesh. Let me take this arrow and shoot it straight at your heart. Imagine some of your not so saved homies roll through while on your road to overcome your alcohol and drug addiction. Like Eve, Satan plants the seed of doubt by saying, "Did God really say you would die if you take a ride with the homies?" Well heck, the way Satan spun it, anyone would have doubt. Entertained by the invitation, uncertainty escorts you to the set up, and you jump into the back seat. Now, because you're in the environment of past familiarities, you hit the blunt, sip on the cognac and bounce to the club. She sees you and you see her, digits are exchanged, passion is exchanged, and you step through the door at 3:00 am. Reader, you have stepped out of the will of God and have granted Satan legal access to your vault. Let's keep it real ladies: dope + alcohol + women = a breach!

Can you hear the alarm going off?

CHAPTER 16: SATAN: THE COUNTERFEIT

If we each look at the design of creation orchestrated by the divine wisdom of God, we will realize that there are spiritual and natural laws to govern and balance the world. When He looked at what He made, He blessed it and said it was very good (Genesis 1:31).

Satan is a created, FALLEN angel (Ezekiel 28:11-19). Satan can never be the Most High God, so he attempts to be "like the Most High God" (Isaiah 14:14). Satan uses deception to alter God's original plan of order. Satan is a counterfeit, and a grand master of illusion (2 Corinthians 11:14). He is a deceiver, promoting false appearances. Satan wants you to believe "a lie" instead of believing the truth about the matter. Remember he always asks the question, "Did God really say that? The scripture provides us more illumination regarding Satan: "Ye are of your father the devil, and the lusts of your father ye will do. He was a murderer from the beginning, and abode not in the truth, because there is no truth in him. When he speaketh a lie, he speaketh of his own: for he is a liar, and the father of it" (Matthew 8:44).

The definition of counterfeit is to forge, copy, and make an imitation of; fraudulent; and imposter, a forgery. For example: (1) The Air sneaker, manufactured in Asia, is a knock-off brand of Nike Air Force 1 (2) Them five-dollar movies sold outta the trunks in the Walmart parking lot, are copies of original movies (3) same-sex unions are a counterfeit and imitation of the original order of marriage ordained by God between a man and woman. Simply put, Satan wants to steal your identity. Listen closely; if you are willingly active in homosexual activities at this very moment, careful, you been "Hacked."

Here is a special report hot off the press. To those of you who proclaim to love Jesus but have not repented of your sins, and confessed Jesus as your personal Lord and Savior, and you are actively and willfully participating in a same-sex relationship, your identity has been stolen and your soul's access to eternal life with Jesus in Heaven is in jeopardy (1 Corinthians 6:9-11).

My brothers and sisters, I pray that this is not you. If it is you, you've been hoodwinked, bamboozled, and betrayed. The Word of God in Galatians 6:7-8 says, "Be not deceived; God is not mocked: for whatsoever a man soweth, that shall he also reap." Verse 8 of Galatians goes on to say, "For he who sows to his own flesh (sexual pleasures) will from the flesh reap decay and ruin and destruction, but he who sows to The Spirit will from The Spirit reap eternal life."

Let me draw back on my bow and arrow and shoot this Gospel game directly at your heart. No matter how short you cut your hair or grow your dread locks, no matter if you play the role of daddy to your partners children, no matter if you dress in men's clothes, talk, sit, stand, dance, drive, eat, "strap on" or change your sex gender, you were born a "WOMAN" and the problem is not with your gender, (female) your struggle is who you see in the MIRROR vs how you are wired in your mind.

Sister, I say this in truth and love. To alter the natural order of God to try to "Be Like" what's in your mind, is to live your life as an imposter and COUNTERFIET.

CHAPTER 17: SYMPTON VS. DISEASE

The definition of disease is a pathological condition of a part, organ or system of an organism resulting from various causes such as infection, genetic defect, or environmental stress and characterized by an identifiable group of signs or symptoms. The definition of symptom is a sign or an indication of disorder or disease, especially when experienced by an individual as a change from normal function, sensation or appearance.

In times past, I attempted to treat the outward manifestations of the sin of homosexuality not knowing that I needed to look inwardly. The spirit of homosexuality was not the root cause but a symptom of a deeper-rooted seed. I would continually pray and bind the spirit of homosexuality, only to discover that the feelings did not pass. In other words, I was not binding the strong man within me.

Let me explain it this way. Americans every year are exposed to the flu. Their symptoms will be sneezing, coughing, fever, headache, etc. These are the outward signs indicating an inward change from the normal function of the body. Every year, pharmaceutical companies profit off thousands of dollars spent on over-the-counter medications to treat the symptoms while medical scientists are still unsuccessful in finding a cure for the flu virus. Sin, just like cancer, not detected early and treated, will kill you.

As I began to examine this revelation that God was birthing in my spirit, I had to ask Him to show me where the door had been opened in my life for Satan to have planted the cancerous seed that within years, infected my perception of gender and steal my identity and inheritance. By God's grace and mercy, He slowly began to rewind the tape of my life and I saw myself as a little child in my parent's room, watching my father's movements and gestures, as he would prepare to go to work. Oh, how I loved and admired my father even to the point of envy. God also allowed me to see clients that I had served and forged relationships with whom I studied to become everything in her brokenness she needed me to be.

Remember, I was a playa, playa, con artist extraordinaire! Aggressive admiration grew into covetousness. Covetousness formed into idolatry.

Idolatry into the worshipping of women. Lusting after women produced sexual acts, and sexual acts produced the manifestation of lesbianism.

Whatever is going on internally, will manifest itself outwardly.
The Word of God says, "For as he thinketh in his heart, so is he" (Proverbs 23:7).

I thought as a man. Therefore, I transformed and functioned as a man.
My dress, conversations and gestures all reflected an inward perception of whom I was contrary to what my gender revealed.

Geneticists believe that within eighteen days, we are either male or female with all the appropriate male and female organs - except for hermaphrodites. In some cases, there are more male hormones in women and more female hormones in men; however, this does not make a convincing case for a baby to be homosexual. I've met several women with wide shoulders, excessive facial hair, and small breasts that play sports, are married to a man, and have children, so let's kill that conspiracy that anatomy leads to lesbianism. Some have professions as doctors; serve in the military as combat fighters, run major corporations, fire fighters, referee for the NFL/NBA, and others are sheriffs who are heterosexual without any desire to be in a same-sex relationship.

Based on my experience and observations, I believe both the scientific evidence and The Word of God: There is no gene or set of biological cells that trigger a male to become female or a female to become male.

There is no little gay gene swimming around in the body that randomly choses who will be gay. No one is born gay. However, some struggle with the mirrors reflection vs their mental wiring. Psychologist have defined this as "Gender Dysphoria." I remember Ms. Oprah Winfrey interviewed Mr. Tyler Perry and while he was being transparent about his molestation, he stated, "When I looked in the mirror, I felt as if my body had betrayed me." I totally understand because when I looked into the mirror, I saw 6' 5" with a penis down to my... Hello!

Satan is clever. The scripture says that he can disguise himself as an angel of light. It also tells us that when he fell, thousands of angels fell with him (Revelations 12:9). That means thousands upon thousands of demonic forces, roaming around, falsely perpetuating themselves as angels of light, are miss leading you into believing you are someone who you are not. This door of deception begins as soon as you can make "free will" choices. In other words, the demons strike in your mind. This is where the battleground for your soul is fought.

Innocence, as in the case of child molestation, child rape, lack of a father's presence and incest; these are fertile grounds for planting the seed of sexual and identity theft. Defenseless children are powerless to protect themselves and as most of these reportable cases indicate, these children when they become adults, have difficulty in sustaining a healthy relationship.

Most of the women that I experienced a homosexual relationship with were heterosexual women who were victims of rape, incest, rejection, abandonment or other forms of molestation at an early age by relatives threatening; that if told, no one would believe them!

Reader, on your road to recovery, I encourage you to carefully visit your childhood and ask The Lord to rewind the tape of your life that will expose Satan and reveal the exact moment that he planted his seed.

Remember, if you continue treating the symptoms, you will prolong finding the cure for the disease.

CHAPTER 18: THE FALSE INHERITANCE

Enticed by the grandeur of promises of power that grant instant pleasure and popularity, and driven by high passions and blind emotions, many of us enter into binding contracts of bondage. These contracts bind us to the agreement, which strongly warn us, that failure to meet the obligations within the contract generally results in added fees, high interest rates, and daily-compounded charges.

Penalties are the section in the contract often brushed over without careful examination of its damaging consequences to our actions.

Satan, who is the Bill Gates of marketing and advertisement, has masterfully designed spiritual contracts that have caught the eye and attention of thousands of Americans throughout the United States. Large corporations who control mass media help to promote Satan's kingdom agenda.

In addition, to pull you in, he uses catch phrases such as no down payment, no credit checks, zero interest rate for one year!

Hells contract allows you to enjoy the merchandise now and pay later.
Hells contract clouds, deceives, and distracts the hidden agenda and true intention of its purpose, which you so quickly skip. Hells contract causes you to forget to read the very fine print located at the bottom of the final page of the contract stating, at the time of your death, I inherit your soul, signed forever yours Satan.

The Word of God says in Psalms 24:1, "The Earth is The Lord's and the fullness thereof the world and they that dwell therein." So, if God owns the whole world, how can Satan promise you what he does not own? The Word of God does say that Satan is the ruler of this world, but ruling does not mean ownership. Ownership means legal right to the possession of a thing.

Let me speak to your spirit women. You may think that right now you are right where you need to be. From where you are looking, you think you have the best seat in the house. You think that right now God is the one blessing you and so enjoying life's pleasures with a woman - you believe God sent. You even claim her to be your soul mate and use catchy phrases like, "She's everything I've always wanted in a man." You may live in the suburbs, house overlooking a lake, swimming pool with an adjacent sauna; mounted 90, 70, and 65 inch flat screens; you may snort prime powder, smoke fluffy purple bud, and drink expensive French cognac; and have a career that justifies the means. You and your partner/wife may have traveled around the world together lounging in 5-star hotels and dining out at prestigious restaurants. You and your partner/wife, according to the State where you reside, adopt kids so you take on the appearance of what society calls the "heterosexual family." You and your partner/wife may attend a local church that condones your lifestyle. However, you may not be aware of this important fact. Satan will bless you to bind you (Mark 8:36).

You can enjoy it temporarily now in your flesh, but you will pay eternally later with your soul. The Word of God says, "For what does it profit a man to gain the world but lose his soul" (Mark 8:36)? All the glamour and glory will all fade away, but God's Word will stand (Isaiah 40:8).

Satan, the David Copperfield of illusion, has taken you like he took Jesus, to an exceedingly high mountain and offered you the fame, the women, entertainment platforms, wealth, swagger, and all the bells and whistles if only you ACCEPT AND BOW to worship him (Mathew 4:1-11).

Sister, you have signed HELLS contract, willfully surrendering your authority, inheritance and salvation to a false god, temporary pleasures, and false inheritance.

Ask me how I know!

CHAPTER 19: HE KNEW ME, HE KNOWS YOU

I wondered how I survived driving back from the Bay Area under the influence of alcohol and drugs to make it home safely. I wondered about all the cocaine and "bud" I smoked, and - how it is that today - I am still in my right mind. (Glory to God!) I wondered about all the women whom I had unprotected sex with, and how I never contracted a sexually transmitted disease. I wondered about the dope houses, the drug deliveries, the weapons, the confrontations on the streets and in the clubs. I wondered why the bullets whizzed by me and hit my friend, paralyzing him. I wonder why my gun refused to discharge the bullet intended for the victim standing within point blank range of my 45. I wondered how an only child was going to survive this world without parents. I wondered about the many friends who did not make it back from the Bay area who are dead and sleeping in their graves.

In an instant and without warning, these men and women never had the chance to repent and get their lives right with Jesus Christ. Many, many nights I paced floors, pondered thoughts and asked God, "Who am I, Lord? Who am I that thou has been so mindful of me?" In addition, like Moses, I asked God how I was going to stand up to Satan and lead a nation of lesbians out of the camps of bondage of their adversary Satan.

I hoped God would let me in on His plan, because I did not have a clue. As always, God spoke to me out of His Holy Word and said, "Before I formed thee in the belly I knew thee, and before thou camest forth out of the womb I sanctified thee and ordained thee a prophet unto the nations" (Jeremiah 1:5). I said to The Lord, "But I am just a child in the ministry.

Lord, I've only preached five times at a local church, and you're putting me up against some heavy hitters politically, socially, and spiritually. God, you are talking about thousands upon thousands of souls." His reply was this, "Say not, I am a child; for thou shalt go to all that I shall send thee, and whatsoever I command thee thou shalt speak. Be not afraid of their faces; for I am with thee to deliver thee, saith The Lord" (Jeremiah 1:7-8).

I said, "Alright then. You go head God, wit yo bad self!

Wonder twins! Power! Activate.

I am an AMBASSADOR FOR CHRIST AND DEFENDER OF THE FAITH!

Finally, I realized that the bitterness, pain, brokenness, anger, rebellion, rejection, and abandonment, and all that the devil tried to use to destroy me, God used it for His divine glory. (Hallelujah!) What I didn't realize then, that I realize now was that I was being trained for a special ops assignment in God's Heavenly boot camp. I was broken to be rebuilt.

Don't get it twisted, many days that I wanted to go AWOL. Nevertheless, there was a press inside of me and a Holy Ghost staff sergeant that would not let me quit. He kept saying, "To him that overcometh will I give to eat of the hidden manna, and will give him a white stone, and in the stone a new name written, which no man knoweth saving he that receiveth it. He that hath an ear let him hear what the spirit is saying to the churches" (Revelation 2:17).

All that I went through, I went through for you. (Selah)

My Sistas, and readers whose hands have turned the pages in this book, not only did God have a plan for my life, He has a plan, purpose and a destiny for yours.

Through it all, Jesus never leaves our side (Genesis 28:15).

I am fully convinced that many souls have seen some difficult times in their lives. But it is the souls that walk through the storm and comesout on the other side by the grace of God that can truly say, "The Lord is my shepherd I shall not want" (Psalm 23:1).

Children of Zion, this book is a mandate from God to you. It's your appointed time and season to be set free. Remember this, "The foundation of God standeth sure having the seal, The Lord knoweth them that are His" (2 Timothy 2:9).

Say this with me, "The Lord knows me."

Now, together, let us take one-step toward freedom, another step toward deliverance, and cross over the bridge to recovery.

CHAPTER 20: THE FIRST STEP

Reader, your courage to read this far is because of the blessing you have received from a Living God, Jehovah Jihra, your provider; Jehovah Nissi, your covering (banner); and, Jehovah Rophe, your Healer who is with you through your exodus of deliverance.

Exodus or (Hodos) is a Greek work, which means departure. The word delivered (Na'al) in Hebrew means to be saved: to be snatched, to pluck out, escape; to be taken out, rescued or recovered.

In the book of Exodus 3:7-8 it reads, "And The Lord said, I have seen the affliction of my people who are in Egypt (where you see the word Egypt, put your city) and have heard their cry because of their task master and oppressors (where you see the word task master put Satan) for I know their sorrows and suffering and trial and I have come down to deliver them out of the hand and power of the Egyptians and to bring them up out of that land (where you see the word land put lifestyle) to a land good and large, a land of plenty." What God is saying is, "I'm ready to deliver you. I'm standing at the door of your heart and I'm knocking." God looks past the symptoms of same-sex attractions and says, "I want to deliver you and pull up the root cause of your pain."

Jesus can speak one word to your circumstance regardless of the appearance and change the out-come of your condition because Jesus (the Anointed one and His Anointing) has the authority, and power to destroy yokes and break the chains of bondage.

Jesus spoke the solution to the problem. He never engaged in any Six Step methodology or billed a client for $150 an hour for counseling sessions. He said to the cripple, "walk." He told the blind to "see." He spoke one word, and they were healed. Jesus wants to restore to you the years, months, days and hours that Satan's demonic strong hold has had over your life. In other words, The Lord wants to give you back what the enemy has stolen from you (Joel 2:25).

The Word of God says that while we were yet sinner's Jesus died for our sins (Romans 5:8).

Jesus loves you. His compassionate grace compels His desire to reach down into the aching place of your heart and touch you were it hurts. There is no place where you have cried that He has not heard you. There is nothing under heaven you've done where the grace of God can't save. He has seen your tears and will wipe them away - all one by one.

I am declaring to you today, Jesus has heard your prayer's regarding your molestation, regarding your rape, regarding your physical and emotional abuse, regarding your drug and alcohol addiction, regarding your feelings of displacement, regarding your feelings of guilt, abandonment and rejection. He is calling you and saying, "Come. I am here."

Reader, I want to sow this deep into your spirit: Jesus loves you! Watch this: Jesus + Deliverance + Recovery = VICTORY! VICTORY! VICTORY!

CHAPTER 21: CONFESSION AND REPENTANCE

I have found that in any aspect of recovery the first step must start with you. You must first be ready to admit that you have a problem. If you have tried like me to deliver you're self from homosexuality, you've probably found yourself within a year relapsing. Jesus needs to perform spiritual surgery on your heart. Allow Him to perform open heart surgery. He has the spiritual forceps to go to the deepest parts of your life and repair the brokenness.

Many folks try to categorize sin. Sin is sin and we must believe and stand upon the truth about what The Word of God says regarding sexual sin. I don't care if it's homosexual or heterosexual sex: Sex outside of the order ordained by God for man and woman in the capacity of marriage, according to The Word of God, is a sin. Period! Dot! The End!

Now when we talk about confession, we are talking about owning or admitting to the truth about a thing. Allow me to assist you in embracing this truth as it applies to the sin of lesbianism. I know you're thinking like, "Jesus loves everyone." and I agree. In John 3:16 it reads, "For God so loved the world that He gave His only begotten Son that WHOSOEVER believeth in Him should not perish, but have everlasting life." The "whosoever" in the verse represents homosexuals, addicts, gang members, adulterers, pimps, hoes, liars, drunkards, murderer's gossipers, etc. Jesus loves you, but Jesus hates the act of sin. He gave us His Son as a gift and the perfect sacrifice to pay the sin debt of Adam's fall.

The chapter of John 3 goes on to say in verse 17, "For God sent not His son into the world to condemn the world; but that the world through Him might be saved." And guess what, He did it while we were yet sinners (Romans 5:8).

Sin has a debt and a penalty attached to it (Romans 6:23). And Jesus carried sin away. He paid for it, and today salvation is the FREE GIFT for the price and penalty of sin (Ephesians 2:8 and Colossians 2:13-14). Jesus was the substitute for us. God's Son, Jesus, carried the sins of the world (yours and mine) (1 Peter 2:24).

Repentance means to turn from your sin/sins. This means that you don't go back and visit that sin any more. To turn simply describes the action. When you turn, you are changing the direction of your previous course.

Exodus happens to be one of my favorite books of The Bible because I can personally relate my life to the history of Israel during their exodus and wilderness journey.

Israel had been in captivity for over 400 years. God used Moses as His instrument and prophet to deliver the people out of the hand of Pharaoh and the bondage of slavery in Egypt.

God purposely harden Pharaoh's heart to demonstrate to the children of Israel that He was JEOVAH Jihre; their provider, who had heard their cries. God was about to perform mightily on their behalf. Pharaoh couldn't accept defeat. With all his wizards, magicians, and pagan gods, they were no match for the great God Jehovah.

As the children of Israel were passing through the waters on their journey to freedom, they heard the sound of Pharaoh's chariots. Moses cast his staff upon the waters and the sea closed and swallowed up Pharaoh's soldiers. The Word of God say's "...and not even one of them remained" (Exodus 14:28).

In this example, God was displaying His ability to do what seemed to be impossible.

Are you catching this reader? God is a way maker. He makes a way out of no way. He takes the impossible and makes it possible. He wants to completely close the door of the bondage of sin in your life.

No matter what your story is or how intricate the details are, Jesus can deliver you. All you need to do is say yes, I'm ready.

Please, will you open the door to your heart and let Him in? Are you ready?

Say this prayer with me:

"Father, in the name of Jesus Christ, I confess that I am a sinner. Lord, I've been out in this world doing too much. I've been practicing in a relationship and leading a lifestyle that is not pleasing to You.

I believe in Your Holy Word Father because Your Word is true.

According to 1 John 1:9, it says that if I confess my sins, You are faithful and just to forgive me of my sins and cleanse me from all unrighteousness.

Father I believe that Jesus lived, died, and was resurrected by You.

Lord Jesus, I need You. I invite You to come into my heart right now. I want You to be The Lord and Savior of my life. I am standing in need of salvation, and according to Your Word, it says that if I confess with my mouth The Lord Jesus, and believe in my heart that God has raised Him from the dead, I shall be saved (Romans 10:9). Now, I thank You Lord for according to Your Word my sins have been forgiven me and I have passed from darkness into your marvelous light (Colossians 1:13)."

The Bible says that the angels in Heaven rejoice over one sinner that repents (Luke 15:10).

Beloved, there is a Holy Ghost party going down on your behalf!

Can you say, "Hey, party over here!"

CHAPTER 22: JUST FOR TODAY

Praise God! Praise God! Praise God!

You have now passed from death (spiritual) to life (eternal) (1 John 3:14).

Now, the journey of recovery begins.

Consider yourself as just coming out of major surgery and resting in the recovery unit where you will begin the rehab process. Remember Sistas, deep wounds and broken bones take time to heal, and Jesus, your rehab specialist has prescribed just the right program for you.

During my journey, I read a book about recovery and three words in a chapter that I read spoke loudly to my spirit. These three words have helped me to deepen my faith and I still carry these words with me. These three words are: Just for Today.

Some women plan their life and set goals as far as five years in advance for projects they need to attain or accomplish. However, for me, along with my identity being stolen, I struggled with my addiction to drugs and alcohol. In 2 Corinthians 12:9, God's Word ministered to me. The words to Paul from God was, "My grace is sufficient for thee, for my strength is made perfect in weakness."

Grace in the Greek means unmerited favor. The word sufficient means more than enough. In essence what God was saying, "Cheryl, My unmerited favor in your circumstance is more than enough and in your weakness, I am strong for you today." When I finally understood that all I needed to do was take hold of the bars of faith, Jesus would be my strength to pull myself up.

Have you ever watched a tag team-wrestling match? One of the wrestlers would fight in the ring getting that butt whooped. The other wrestler would know their partner needed help. So, they would stretch their hand out to be tagged in. Well, Jesus is leaning on the ropes of your life right at this moment screaming, "TAG ME! TAG ME! TAG ME INTO YOUR LIFE! Watch Me perform on your behalf."

If you're anything like me, I had control issues, so trust and letting go of the wheel did not come easy. I've learned however that in my brokenness and weakness, Jesus is my strength.

Every day I was beginning to realize that when Cheryl got out of the way, Jesus could step in and do the work in me that I couldn't possibly do myself. When Cheryl's pride, logic, and analytical reasoning decreased, His divine wisdom increased.

Your faith must be anchored in knowing that "Just for Today" God can, has, and will, supply all your needs according to His riches and glory in Heaven (Philippians 4:19).

Life will show up and the enemy will be persistent in harassing you. TRUST!

Remember, the enemy's assignment is to kill, steal, and destroy. He has the legal right for a season to interfere with your recovery (salvation). Satan will bring people, places, and things in your life to remind you of who you used to be. In addition, from my own experience, people will try to hold you in bondage to your past in spite of what The Lord has done. Do not believe the lie of the enemy. Do not bite the bait. Say to the Devil, "You are a liar and I stand firm in the freedom of which I have been called." Tell him sis, say, "Just for today I can do all things in Christ which strengthens me" (Philippians 4:13). Gird yourself up girl and proclaim, "I am more than a conquer and no weapon that is formed against me shall prosper."

My friends, you must learn to speak God's Word over your life every day, every hour and every minute while you are walking through your recovery. God's word is the prescription for your breakthrough.

CHAPTER 23: CO-DEPENDENCY

I pray that as we walk through the final pages of this book that you pay particular attention to the last words of The Holy Spirit as He reveals His grace in guiding you to your breakthrough. The Word of God says that you shall know the truth and the truth shall set you free (John. 8:32).

Let's break down the word co-dependency. The prefix co- means in cooperation with. The word dependency or dependent means relying on or requiring the aid of another for support. It's also known as relationship dependency.

Let's put it all together so it fits the subject matter of this chapter regarding co-dependent lesbian relationships. Lesbian co-dependency is two women in a relationship cooperatively relying on and requiring the aid of one another for support.

Emotion is defined as intense feelings such as love, hate or despair. So if one woman brings this intensity of emotions, imagine the impact of two women living together under the same roof? This intensity would be magnified to 10th power. And, Baby, let's not even discuss if one or both women are in the age of menopause. Co-dependency robs you of your unique individuality, integrity and humility.

A woman, who is co-dependent, usually has very low self-esteem and searches for everything outside herself to make the situation feel better.

Through my experience as a lesbian in a co-dependent relationship, I have come to realize that co-dependency engrafts you into your partner physically, mentally, and spiritually. For example, you will begin to lose your individuality and uniqueness in the relationship. Co-dependents are rescuers. This co-dependency is from a root of deception.

I feel like a filmmaker right now, so let me take out my spiritual camera and roll this clip for you.

The spirit of deception in a lesbian relationship sinks its talons deep into your mind and whispers in your ear that you can't live, breathe or function without this woman. Slowly, he strategically plants this image (seed) in your mind and as it begins to take root, you find yourself saying things like, "I'll kill somebody who tries to come in between us baby," or "I'll kill you if you ever try to leave me." Both of you chuckle at these statements, but as you release each other from the embrace, one of you is not playing. You'll even notice that you are becoming jealous over her friends, family, coworkers, new car, knew hairstyle and now have become a private detective of her personal affairs. Your overbearing ways and exploits of jealous overtures become the main topic of many intense arguments.

Jealousy, now fully matured, has transformed into rage, and rage when it has fully reached its boiling point, burst forth like a consuming combustion of fire destroying and murdering everything in its path.

Unable to contain the fiery rages, and unaware of your actions, you find yourself standing in the middle of your kitchen, heart racing, as you realize your hand is gripping the blood-stained knife, as your eyes behold the lifeless corpse of your partner lying in a pool of blood.

Cut!

This imagery is not a trailer snippet of a horror flick or a movie on "Lifetime." This imagery is real talk readers. The reality in this story is that hundreds of lesbians tragically contribute to the percentage of victims and assailers of domestic violence.

Ladies, (I'm directly talking to lesbians) this may not be your personal testimony or your expected end. But, if you are living in a same-sex relationship you can honestly agree, if I'm not on your street, or driving in your hood, I'm in the vicinity.

Honk! Honk! Beep! Beep!

The spirit of deception is a strong and ancient demon. Remember, deception deceived Eve in the Garden.

I must address this to the church. If you are living in a lifestyle that is not pleasing to God, and you are walking in disobedience, I want to caution you that disobedience is an open door for Satan to plant seed and raise havoc in your life and ministry!

Readers, I'm still hearing the voice of The Lord telling me to say, "Keep it real Cheryl and tell the whole story." So, I must obey and keep the proverbial cameras rolling.

This imagery is a backdrop for the next scene. Roll'em on two...ACTION!

This account is a true factual event of a co-dependent relationship that entangled me, and another sister who was a leader in ministry. To keep her name confidential I will call her Sista Cornbread.

I was dating Sista Cornbread and when we met, I had a substantial savings account, a credit score of 700, and a furnished apartment. I listened to Gospel music, ate healthy foods, drove a BMW, had a good paying job; never smoked cigarettes, and hadn't touched a drop of alcohol in two years. But, all of that didn't matter because all I knew was that Sista Cornbread was fine!

Sista Cornbread had a bodacious body, eyes that hypnotized, and a melodic voice that was angelic. The more time Sista Cornbread and I spent together, the more I began to compromise my individuality. I began telling myself, "So what if I told all my homies and made several vows after the fourth, five, and sixth painful break-up stating that I'll never date straight women. So, what if she smokes a little bit. Three or four cigarettes ain't too bad. So what if she is in between jobs and needs to borrow money for her rent. So what if she doesn't want to go out in public with me and only desires to see me after dark at my crib. So what! Sista Cornbread is fine."

After six months of this cat and mouse courtship, I avoided the two-year rule and moved Sista Cornbread into my crib.

At church I tried to conceal my feelings, but of course, I had the "I'm knockin' her boots off grin."

After a while, the melodic Gospel rhythms that saturated my apartment faded.

I found myself spending crazy cash to impress Sista Cornbread.

The man mentality was rising. I had to prove my ability to be Mr. Provider and Super Stud. I had to be the man who took care of all her needs. At the same time, I was unaware that my savings account had almost depleted.

One day, I passed by a mirror and said to myself, "Boy, I've lost a lot of weight." The mirror reflected the sunken-in cheek bones of what used to be a healthy round face.

Sista Cornbread and I laughed it off as I made jokes about her bulging clavicle bone that was not noticeable when you first met.

Driving for late night dope runs in the wee morning crack hours, and pulling "All Niters", became the theme of our relationship. The party that started at 6:00 p.m. is winding down with the rising of the 6:00 a.m. sun.

Soon the heartfelt vow of my eternal love to Sista Cornbread came crashing in, as I attempted to hide my crack addiction.

Early in the morning, while sleeping my high off, I was awakened by the property owner knocking at the door. She served us the three-day eviction notice. My eyes still hazy from the dope party just hours before, I held it in disbelief. I closed the door with the notice in my hand, I gazed down at the frail frame of a woman who once had the most bodacious body, angelic voice, beautiful eyes, curled up at the foot of the king size mattress which was the only reminder of your once furnished apartment.

CUT!!!!!

I'm on somebodies street now.

Right now, as I'm writing these words, I can hear The Spirit of The Lord say, "Arise and awake my sleeping children, Behold, I come quickly."

The deceptive spirit operating behind co-dependency tells you that all though you and Sister Cornbread are addicts, flat broke and homeless, you could save each other and pull each other out of the pit of hell that you both have fallen into.

Ladies, wake up! Come forth from your chambers of deception. The devil is a liar.

I've come to declare to you today that because the power of God brought me out, I've been sent as a witness to stop by your hood, by way of the pages in this book, to testify, and inform you that the only person that can go to hell, and bring you out, is the only person that conquered hell and that is Yeshua Hamaschiach, Jesus Christ The Lord!

Yeshua is the KING of KINGS; The Great "I AM" and The LORD of LORDS. His name is above every name in Heaven, Earth and beneath the Earth. (Selah)

The Holy Spirit is so awesome in His timing.

Before penning the final words in this chapter; I was at the car wash vacuuming out my car and listening to this gospel CD. The words of this song are a perfect climax for this portion of the book.

I believe it went a little bit like this (thank God I don't have to sing it to you, for I've learned in ministry to stay in my lane) it said, "I'm reaping the harvest God has for me, take back what the devil stole from me and I rejoice today, that I shall recover it all."

I said, "That's it God, part of the journey of recovery is taking back what the enemy has stolen from us" and now that we have right standing with Christ according to the shedding of His blood, and a repentant heart, we can rightfully claim our inheritance.

I know folks at the car wash thought I was about one gene short of being a 51/50 patient, but I didn't care. I gave God a good 'ole Apostolic, Church of God in Christ, Pentecostal shout! I mean, I gave him a crazy praise.

I can feel the anointing of God upon me right now and it's time that we set it off.

Sistas, roll up your sleeves, pull your hair back, stand in your authority and mount up! It's time to march into the enemy's camp and serve notice to the devil. Say this with me, "Satan, I rebuke you! I command you in the name of Jesus Christ that you loose everything you stole from me.

Give me back my life.
Give me back my identity.
Give me back my peace of mind.
Give me back my joy and laughter.
Release my finances.

Release my ministry.
Release my children.
Release my femininity.
Release my husband (He is coming sis).

Satan you're a player hater and I don't belong to you because I come from God's stock. I'm a joint heir with Jesus Christ, and I sit with Him in Heavenly places, and just in case you forgot who I am, I'm the daughter of the Most High God EL ELyon and I decree and declare to you today that I am free for whom The Lord has set free, is FREE INDEED! In the name of Jesus!"

Girl go get your stuff!

CHAPTER 24: FROM BOXERS TO PANTIES?

Walking into a woman's dressing room, trying on women's clothing was not the business; let alone, learning to re-button a woman's shirt from the left to the right.

I defiantly know how awkward it is when you realize women's pants do not have five deep pockets for your Louis Vuitton wallet.

Please let me encourage you. Don't get overwhelmed and discouraged by attempting a "Glamour Girl" makeover. Keep your swag, swing your dreads, don't be ashamed of your tattoos and rock your Air Force 1's.

Your outer transformation, if led by the grace of God, will not be overnight, so Sista, give yourself a break and just breathe.

Paul writes in Romans12:2a, "...Be not conformed to this world: but be ye transformed by the renewing of your mind..." not the renewing of your swag. I'm confident that Jesus is more concerned with your soul and not your clothes.

Jesus wants to restore and more importantly, will remove the appearance of the old you, and that begins in your heart and mind.

God's grace is an amazing experience. Grace enables us to do what we are unable to do. If you allow Him this wonderful opportunity, you will find that in time, not even the residue of your former lifestyle will be noticeable. (Thinking, actions, conversations.)

You might be asking, "How do I renew my mind Cheryl?" Well, that's an excellent question sis and I am so glad you asked. The answer is relationship. You've been chasing temporary fulfillment and Jesus wants to end the cycle of discouragement and disappointment. CHASE AFTER HIM! Becoming intimate with Christ is the greatest love affair you can ever experience. The more time you spend in fellowship with God and His Word, the more of His Holy Spirit will dwell in you, and before you know it, the former things will fade away.

Take your recovery one day, one hour and one second at a time and I promise you, before you realize it, maybe, your boxers will turn into panties.

CHAPTER 25: A SOUND FROM HEAVEN

Addressing lesbian, transgender, and bisexual women all over the nation reading this book.

I've seen you in my spirit, my dreams and my visions. I've seen you in your jail cells, cafes, coffee shops, bus stops, trains, airports, break rooms, living rooms, bedrooms, class rooms, cars, trucks and SUV's.

In my spirit, I have heard the chains of bondage being broken, and seen the tears of release flowing down your cheeks. I speak total restoration of God's transformation in your life. I speak God's perfect will and perfect purpose being fulfilled today in your lives. I decree and declare freedom, triumph and healing within your soul in the name of Jesus.

Arise, arise, beautiful Queens! You all are the daughters of The King, and for the rest of your lives walk in your royal inheritance.

Addressing the priest in God's house and those who watch, pray and shepherd God's flock.

I earnestly pray that my truthful testimony will be the cornerstone for your understanding and as you stand in your pulpits, and walk onto your platforms, please remember that the homosexuals that walk into your sanctuary could be your next evangelist, pastor or prophet.

Addressing the entertainment industry.

Come out, come out wherever you are.

Every singer, rapper, actor, actress, athlete, talk show host, on TV or radio, God says come out!

I speak and declare that you shall no more be deceived by the spirit of Babylon in Jesus name. Be free and come forth! There is rest in Christ for your soul. Drink from His fountain and never be thirsty. Take from His Word the bread from Heaven that is plentiful and everlasting.

Addressing men and women on the down-low.

When you return to your wife or husband; to your children, families, friends and churches; after laying with your lover and thinking nobody saw you in the restaurant, leaving the motel and getting into your car... Surprise.... Jesus did! He saw you!

The eyes of The Lord are everywhere!

Be not deceived, for God is not mocked for whatsoever a man/woman soweth that shall he/she also reap (Galatians 6:7). Reap everlasting life and not death.

Stand up and gird your loins with The Word of Truth and depart from the exhausting years of living a double lifestyle.

I speak into your life and break the power of the Satan's demonic ambassadors, their assignment to kill, still, destroy, and the door that was open for him to plant his seed.

I take my spiritual ax and I come against the root of its fulfillment. I decree that today and for the rest of your life you shall walk Holy as healed men and women of God in Jesus name, Amen.

Sisters, my heart's desire and prayer for God for you is that you might be saved.

Love,

Your Sister and servant in Christ,
Cheryl Weston
Samuel and Mary Weston's Baby Girl